Value-led Organizations

Eleanor Bloxham

- Fast track route to understanding value led organizations

- Covers the key areas of value leadership, from developing critical measurement and compensation practices to evaluating changing environmental, global, and social impacts and establishing sound corporate governance

- Examples and lessons from some of the world's most successful businesses, including Berkshire Hathaway, Odey Asset Management, Halma, and Honda, and ideas from the smartest thinkers, including Warren Buffet, Richard Brealey, Peter Koestenbaum, William Mahoney and Roger Raber

- Includes a glossary of key concepts and a comprehensive resources guide

essential management thinking at your fingertips

First published 2002 by
Capstone Publishing (a Wiley company)
8 Newtec Place
Magdalen Road
Oxford OX4 1RE
United Kingdom
http://www.capstoneideas.com

CIP catalogue records for this book are available from the British Library and the US Library of Congress

ISBN 1-84112-310-2

This book is printed on acid-free paper

Contents

Introduction to ExpressExec

ExpressExec is 3 million words of the latest management thinking compiled into 10 modules. Each module contains 10 individual titles forming a comprehensive resource of current business practice written by leading practitioners in their field. From brand management to balanced scorecard, ExpressExec enables you to grasp the key concepts behind each subject and implement the theory immediately. Each of the 100 titles is available in print and electronic formats.

Through the ExpressExec.com Website you will discover that you can access the complete resource in a number of ways:

» printed books or e-books;
» e-content – PDF or XML (for licensed syndication) adding value to an intranet or Internet site;
» a corporate e-learning/knowledge management solution providing a cost-effective platform for developing skills and sharing knowledge within an organization;
» bespoke delivery – tailored solutions to solve your need.

Why not visit www.expressexec.com and register for free key management briefings, a monthly newsletter and interactive skills checklists. Share your ideas about ExpressExec and your thoughts about business today.

Please contact elound@wiley-capstone.co.uk for more information.

Introduction to Value-led Organizations

- » A number of changes are impacting on organizations today including;
  - » increased stakeholder activism;
  - » technological enhancements;
  - » higher levels of personal investment;
  - » greater informational requirements;
  - » globalization; and
  - » stronger scrutiny of board practices.
- » These changes are creating a need for organizations to clarify their values, purposes, and goals.
- » There are increasing external pressures on organizations from shareholders, regulators, and employees to be value-led.
- » It is important that organizations understand what it means to be value-led and to seek out a number and variety of role models.

As stakeholder activism has increased and technology has made information both more timely and more available, the pressures on organizations to become value-led have intensified. In the US, organizations and analysts alike are being pushed to provide more information, on a timely basis, to a variety of constituents. This pressure for increased information, sometimes called "transparency," is generally focused on allowing the markets, and other constituents, greater access to information concerning the internal operations of the organization.

There are historical reasons for this change. Across the world, many of the paternalistic practices of the depression and post-depression years are giving way to greater financial literacy and self-sufficiency. These changes mean that individuals are taking more responsibility for their investments and retirement savings. As a result, the requirements for useful information have increased. With this change, it has become even more important that organizations clarify their values, their purposes and their goals, not only for internal purposes, but also to satisfy external constituents.

With globalization and technological changes have come increased complexities for both profit and non-profit organizations. These complexities have made it necessary for organizations to understand more fully their relationships with stakeholders on a number of dimensions. These dimensions include the creation of value for their shareholders (or other funding sources), the satisfaction of customer needs, and the productive use of human and other forms of capital in a way that is cognizant of both long-term stewardship and environmental, community, and global concerns.

Clearly defining values along all of these dimensions is more complicated than ever, but the pressure to do so has never been greater.

One major source of pressure to become value-led has been from regulatory agencies. Regulations requiring organizational transparency have created a strong need for enhanced organizational self-examination. For example, in the US, recent regulations have modified established accounting standards, including reporting requirements for business segments, to promote greater scrutiny of an organization's internal operations by outsiders. And currently, the NASD (National Association of Securities Dealers) is considering a proposal to require public disclosure by analysts and brokerage firm employees of their personal ownership in stocks they recommend. And to disclose any conflicts of interest within their firms that could potentially bias their opinions. Such disclosure requirements are simply part of a recent trend in providing investors (funding sources) with the information needed to determine, legitimately, which organizations are, in fact, creating value. Similarly, US government organizations have been required, under the Government Performance and Results Act of 1993, to report to Congress on their performance using a number of metrics designed to aid in making the same determination.

During an interview with Bill Mahoney, executive editor of *Shareholder Value Magazine*, the author was asked to explain these new pressures: In addition to regulatory, "there is pressure from the market. There is also pressure from inside companies, namely, the new generation of managers who . . . are willing to change an organization to one that represents good value from [an] ethics and communications standpoint." ("Heading into a sea of change," *Shareholder Value Magazine* March–April 2001.)

The topic of value-led organizations becomes increasingly important as organizations respond to these challenges and to a landscape that includes new shareholder activist organizations, vigorous analyses by pension fund managers, growing shareholder litigation, and stronger scrutiny of board practices. The topic is more important because role models are needed. Being value-led, as "Value-led Organizations" will discuss, is multidimensional. Just as individuals may be especially talented in one area and less so in others, the same is true for value-led organizations. As clear an understanding as possible is needed by every organization to understand what it takes to be value-led, and to support the need to seek out a number and variety of role models. Of course, these role models will evolve over time as changes occur and awareness evolves. Despite those changes, however, the subject of value-led organizations will always be important to those who care and wish to improve the way organizations are governed.

What is a Value-led Organization?

- » A value-led organization focuses on value.
- » A value-led organization manages for value.
- » Stewardship or care is the hallmark for value leadership.
- » Value leadership applies to all types of organizations.
- » The principles of value leadership are long-standing.
- » Being value-led is multidimensional.
- » Value-led organizations strive to be value-led in as pervasive and integrative a way as possible.
- » In reality, not all value-led organizations are value-led in every dimension at all times.

BEING VALUE-LED: THE IDEAL

A value-led organization is an organization focused on value – focused on creating it and focused on sustaining it. There is an ethical dimension implied by the term "value-led." Unfortunately, those less familiar with value concepts and their power to transform have weakened this dimension.

Value-led organizations manage for value. In October 1998, the *Journal of Strategic Performance Measurement* devoted the entire issue to the subject of value. In an article entitled "Why value management.", the author explains that value leadership "is an integrated approach to managing any organization. It is based on the principle of stewardship (and the inexorable consequences of failed stewardship)."

Value-led organizations manage in a holistic fashion, with awareness, and take their fiduciary duties seriously. Stewardship or care is the hallmark of value-leadership.

Value-leadership is not limited to business entities listed on the world's stock exchanges. Value-led organizations can include government, quasi-government, non-profit, or profitable endeavors. Profitable firms may be privately or publicly held. The hallmark of all these organizations, however, is that they exercise stewardship or care over all the resources entrusted to them.

Despite its broader applicability, the *primary* references to value-led or value-managed relate to the exercise of stewardship with respect to their funding, i.e. their capital. Discussions about stewardship and its importance have been recognized for hundreds of years. This kind of stewardship, for example, is discussed in the Biblical story of the master and his servants called "The Parable of the Ten Minas" in Luke 19:11 (and in Matthew 25:14 called "The Parable of the Talents"). In these stories, a master gives money to servants, placing it in their care while he is away. From Luke: "He called ten of his servants and gave them ten minas. 'Put this money to work,' he says 'until I come back.' Upon his return, the master asks of each servant what they have done during his absence. The first servant says, 'Sir, your mina has earned ten more.' The second servant says, 'Sir, your mina has earned five more.' In gratitude and praise, the master gives them each cities to command. Then another servant comes back to the master and says, 'Sir, here is your mina. I have kept it laid away in a piece of cloth.' The master replies: 'Why then didn't you put my money on deposit so that when I came back, I could have collected interest? Take his mina away from him and give it to the one who has ten minas.' '[1] Capital, market, and stewardship lessons are all encapsulated in one simple story.

Value-led organizations recognize and consciously act on the responsibility to provide a return to those who invest in them. Although these concepts are usually discussed in the context of profit-centered businesses, they are also more generally applicable. In *The Quest for Value*, Bennett Stewart describes it this way:

> "A quest for value directs scarce resources to their most promising uses and most productive users ... Adam Smith's invisible hand is at work when the investor's private gain turns into a public virtue. Although there are exceptions to this rule, most of the time there is a happy harmony between creating stock market value and enhancing the quality of life."
>
> *G. B. Stewart III, The Quest for Value, New York: Harper Collins, 1991*

Stewart eloquently connects the focus on value to its ultimate rewards. Value-leadership benefits the shareholder; but it also benefits society as a whole. This concept is critical to understanding the nature of value in the larger context – and stewardship as a specific act. This need for stewardship is applicable to all enterprises.

To manifest their objectives of stewardship, value-led organizations take on a number of activities. One activity is the development of metrics to help the organization understand whether it has created or destroyed value. Before the advent of value metrics, the ability to manage a complex organization for value was limited by the inability to measure the results of its actions from a value perspective. A value-led organization understands its purpose and measures the value it has created with the funding it has received.

Another activity of value-led organizations is the adoption of value principles and metrics in the strategic planning process. Strategy is driven by value concepts and choosing among alternative strategic approaches with an understanding of the value impacts. In addition to using value metrics to inform and select strategies, the strategy itself may dictate the value measures the organization may wish to monitor on an ongoing basis. Roy Johnson, who directed the efforts of Pitney Bowes to integrate value-based performance into a corporate-wide financial planning system, has written that:

> "Financial drivers . . . should be an integral part of a comprehensive value-based system . . . The business strategy will often determine the prioritization and emphasis for specific financial drivers."
> *"Getting it right: a template for creating real value,"*
> *Shareholder Value Magazine, March–April 2001*

An important activity for value-led organizations is the integration of value metrics into the human capital planning and compensation processes. As organizations have become increasingly dependent on intellectual capabilities to succeed, a focus on human capital has emerged. Value-led organizations, as good stewards of all capital, have been at the forefront of responsible management of this important resource. In the *Journal of Cost Management*, in November 2000 the author wrote:

> "Managing human capital investments is an issue of measurement and mindset. . . the market attempts to quantify, intuitively or otherwise, the future value of intangibles."
> *"Intangibles: human capital and options value measurement"*

Value-led organizations create value by using human capabilities responsibly and productively. Mark Ubelhart, in an article entitled "Measuring the immeasurable", wrote: "Of course, there is intuitive support for the notion that engaged employees are more likely to enhance value creation as reflected in the capital markets. 'Best employer' lists often correlate with best financial results." (*Shareholder Value Magazine*, May–June 2001.)

Value-led organizations naturally take the processes and activities required to be value-led very seriously. Of course, to do all of the above, value-led organizations must start with an understanding of their mandate as fiduciaries. Peter Koestenbaum, in an interview with Polly Labarre entitled "Do you have the will to lead?" in *Fast Company* magazine in March 2000, suggests that, in the decisions of individuals as well as organizations, it is the intention, understanding, and dialogue that matter. For value-leaders, this intention and dialogue relate to the mission of creating value and they are central to every activity of the organization. It is no longer good enough only to have satisfied customers or employees. The mission must include responsibility to a larger group without whom the organization could not thrive. This larger group, consisting of shareholders, employees, customers, suppliers, and even the surrounding communities, must be considered in the decision-making process. Being value-led is integrating. A value-led organization clarifies goals and objectives; strives to create value; and exercises responsibility and stewardship in all that it does.

Ideally, being value-led is not a minor part of a value-led organization's activity. It is pervasive as well as integrative. Everyone in the organization understands it. (Training is very important to success.) And everyone understands the value of being value-led – experientially. The organization communicates itself to others in value-led terms. And the language of value creation and stewardship is used throughout the organization.

BEING VALUE-LED: THE REALITY

This said, more often than not, authors discuss value as if perfection existed. In fact, however, one reason for cynicism about value-led organizations is the lack of realism. Just as Tom Peters, author of *In Search of Excellence*, found in studying firms, a company may be quite excellent in one dimension or for a certain period of time, and less so in another dimension or at another point in time. As with excellent companies, it is also true for value-led organizations. The stamina, strength, capacity, and understanding to be value-led in many dimensions over long periods of time are overwhelming for most firms. To find appropriate value-led role models, it is important to recognize that an organization still may be considered to be value-led even if it is value-led:

» in one or a few dimensions only;
» at certain times only (during its history);
» to a greater or lesser extent on any given dimension.

Understanding and accepting the reality (while seeking to change and improve it), is critical to the ability of value-led organizations to make progress and develop internal bench strength. Being a value-led organization is not a yes or no concept. As will be explained in the case studies in Chapter 7, one hallmark of value-led organizations is that they admit their mistakes – and make changes as a result of them.

Being value-led, then, represents a continuum. Organizations can vary in the number of dimensions in which they are value-led. They may be value-led in their work with customers. This may be seen, for example, in ensuring that customers are not harmed by their products. Or they may be value-led in terms of metrics and use those metrics to understand (much better than their competitors) when value is created in their organization or by others in their industry.

A value-led organization may be more value-led at certain times in its history than others. Perhaps it exercises extreme stewardship at the beginning when funding is tight, loses track of these principles as it develops, and then comes back to them when times are tough. Or perhaps a new leader comes to the firm (as is the recent case with Kmart discussed in Chapter 7) determined to create a value-led organization. (Or a leader may come determined to *remove* the focus from value principles.)

A value-led organization may vary in the extent to which it is value-led on any dimension. One value-led organization, for example, may only develop high-level value creation metrics and no measures of value creation at the product or customer level. Another may develop not only high-level metrics for itself and its competitors, but also measures at every level of the organization. Companies may even develop measures of value, not only *about* customers, but also *for* the use of customers in their own businesses. In all these ways, although the framework is consistent, what a value-led organization may demonstrate can vary considerably.

Bill Mahoney, executive editor of *Shareholder Value Magazine*, puts it this way:

"Smart investors want corporate managers to work for their customers, seek to bolster productivity and optimize the benefits of alliances. These are key ways shareholder value is created. . .

Shareholder value isn't fading as a mantra for running a business. It's growing up."

"Defining shareholder value," Shareholder Value Magazine,
October–November 2000

In the interview with Bill Mahoney "Heading into a sea of change", already quoted above, on what is involved in becoming value-led, the author says:

"Recognizing the value of an economic profit framework is the first recognition. It's the easiest step . . . The deeper understanding comes from embracing the notion that if we actually go forward, it will fundamentally change the way we do business. We're going to be making decisions in a different way . . . Many benefits accrue . . . Companies that truly put it in place are going to have a competitive advantage . . . And value management is an integration of a number of disciplines, all coming together to make it work."

NOTE

1 *The Holy Bible*, New International Version, Grand Rapids, MI: Zondervan Publishing House, 1984.

The Evolution of Value Concepts for Organizations

» The evolution of value concepts for organizations comes from diverse sources.
» Corporate finance, risk analyses, business ethics and business law, financial and management accounting are all important disciplines with implications for value-led organizations.
» Miller, Modigliani, Markowitz, Sharpe, Black, and Scholes are some of the pioneers of value-related concepts in corporate finance.
» GM and GE were very early adopters in the 1920s and 1950s respectively of value-based metrics and compensation concepts.

Many can claim a piece of the ownership of ideas surrounding the evolution of value-led organizations. Because the concepts and applications touch a number of diverse disciplines and contexts, so the origins too come from a number of diverse sources.

One source of many of the concepts is found in the principles of modern corporate finance. These include net present value, the role of capital, asset pricing, valuation, and options theory. (These terms are defined in the glossary in Chapter 8.)

M&M GIVE US SOMETHING TO CHEW ON

In 1958[1] and 1961,[2] Franco Modigliani and Merton Miller published articles that discussed the nature of capital. They argued that the value of a firm is not based on the structure or form of its capital, but on the value created or generated by using the capital in any form. In other words, all other things being equal, the value of a firm is the same whether the capital is in the form of debt or equity, as long as there are no other factors related to the structure that affect cash flow (transaction costs and tax effects are examples of such factors). An understanding of valuation and cost of capital is important to value-led organizations. These fundamental principles lead to the recognition of one of the keys to managing a firm on a value basis: that both debt and equity have a quantifiable cost. Although the cost of equity is not reflected on the income statement or balance sheet, it is a true cost and value-led firms recognize it. (In fact, due to the tax effect, debt may be a less costly form of capital than equity.) This valuation analysis is also important because it creates a process for thinking about the separation of operational and financing decisions. It places the focus on the one that makes a real difference in an organization's value creation – operations. This framework also provides a way of thinking about the value of each operation and for valuing different organizations with different capital structures.

SHARPE-NING THE THEORY

In corporate finance, the CAPM (capital asset pricing model) represents a further breakthrough in valuing assets and developing discount rates. Its development was based on work by Henry Markowitz. CAPM was introduced by William Sharpe in 1964.[3] It is important to organizations in providing a way to think about the cost of capital. To be value-led, organizations need to have a method for quantifying this cost, and the CAPM offers one approach.

The CAPM estimates the cost of capital to be the risk-free rate plus beta (the stock's systematic risk) multiplied by the market risk premium (the rate of return of the market less the risk-free rate). Many academics argue over the inherent difficulties in determining the inputs to the CAPM. However, many organizations value the CAPM for its usefulness in sorting out the relative values of alternative scenarios in making decisions. (Those organizations not concerned with valuation continue to use payback or other non-rigorous methods.) While theories surrounding the cost and use of capital are continually evolving, the concepts presented by Modigliani, Miller, Markowitz, and Sharpe provide major pieces of the framework used by value-led organizations.

BLACK & SCHOLES KEEP YOUR OPTIONS AFLOAT

The latest frontier has been in the area of options theory. In 1973, Fischer Black and Myron Scholes developed a method to price financial options using information about the relationship between time, volatility, the underlying value of the security, and the risk free rate of return.[4] This model was developed as an equilibrium model for pricing stock options. The applications for value-led organizations are twofold. Corporate finance has expanded the use of these models beyond the pricing of financial derivatives to providing a thought process for thinking about business options. Work in this area continues to expand as new theories and applications are being developed. (See also Chapter 6 for a discussion of this and its implications for the future.) The second use of options pricing is in quantifying the value of options used in incentive plans. Its use has proliferated to the point that even organizations not using the information to make value-based decisions must, from a practical standpoint, understand the calculations. Members of boards of directors with no corporate finance background must, from a good governance standpoint in value-led organizations, understand the applicability of the other corporate finance principles as well as options pricing theories, in order to fulfil their responsibilities related to strategic planning and compensation effectively.

As in all endeavors, practice lags behind theory. The time from availability to adoption of new approaches can be twenty to thirty years or more. Value-led organizations are early adopters of recognized thought processes that are not yet in mainstream use. Since value-led organizations may be value-led in certain aspects of the business and not in others, they may be early adopters in certain areas and not others. Some organizations may also move in and out of being value-led – dependent on their management, their boards, and their true understanding of the concepts.

RISK ANALYSES

Where corporate finance and statistics merge in the area of risk analysis, there lies another foundation for the "innerwork" of value-led organizations. This intersection involves the measurement of volatility (variation) and risk – diversifiable and not. This is a subject of great academic interest. Value-led organizations use this information extensively to understand their operations and their investments. The information value of this analysis is often overlooked or ignored by organizations that are not value-led. Its value in strategic decision-making is so great that value-led organizations often use it as a key first step.

BUSINESS ETHICS, BUSINESS LAW AND GENERAL BUSINESS PRACTICE

Another foundation point for value-led organizations is the study of business ethics and business law. The halls of academia are littered with case studies and examples of firms who did not carefully examine the consequences of their decision-making processes; who did not define their standards and values early on; who did not ensure that everyone in the organization understood and used them. These examples lead to the recognition of the need for training and communication in value-led organizations at levels not previously identified.

FINANCIAL AND MANAGEMENT ACCOUNTING

Financial and management accounting are other areas of importance in terms of the evolution of value-led organizations. Financial accounting and strict standards of reporting are critical to value-led organizations from several standpoints. One area is fair reporting to shareholders. The standards help value-led organizations develop a consistency and honesty of reporting that is important to them. Value-led organizations tend to report more than required, rather than less. The development of standard accounting principles provides a firm foundation that value-led organizations can draw upon.

Another reason that evolution in this arena is so important to value-led organizations is in their competitive analyses and partnering decisions. Without strong financial standards, information about one's own business is not only less sure in the minds of shareholders, it also makes it difficult for organizations to understand whether to enter a business, purchase another company, or sell a division. In areas of the world where standards are less strict, this information cost is reflected in the cost of capital.

The "information effect" on cost of capital and the ability to attract capital are other reasons value-led organizations go beyond the standards in reporting. In the US, the first accounting standards were promulgated in the 1930s as a result of the market crash. Ever since, there has been a steady stream of updates and clarifications. Recently, very significant additions have been made. In June of 1997, for example, FAS (Financial Accounting Standard) 131 required companies to provide documented financials not only for the company as a whole but also for the distinct business areas the company manages.

This reporting requirement was important in signaling that shareholders require more information to make judgments about firms and that this information should meet agreed standards.

Many value-led organizations have reported the information for years in advance of the requirement. The requirement, however, has been part of an increased awareness of the services that shareholders expect and require. The call for increasing transparency is an important part of this, and the evolution in terms of these requirements continues. (See Chapter 7 for examples of value-led organizations that have exceeded requirements in reporting.)

The evolution of management as opposed to financial accounting has also been important to value-led organizations. Business unit reporting and costing methodologies have been important in understanding the value created by relevant parts of the business, its divisions and products. CRM, or customer relationship management, has been a more recent offshoot of these endeavors.

Management accounting practices have also been important in the area of budgeting and annual planning. Before the advent of computers, these processes were performed manually. As a result, forecasts and updates were performed at a very high level. With the advent of computers, and particularly personal computers in the 1980s, organizations were able to quantify the information more quickly and, most importantly, perform what-if analyses. Although the structure of the budgeting processes remained much the same, more iterations at a more detailed level of analysis were possible.

In the 1990s, value-led organizations began to re-examine some of the arbitrary structures that had evolved as calendar planning processes, in part due to the lack of technology to do otherwise. These firms began to implement rolling plans and to use value-based techniques in their processes.

RAPPAPORT & STEWART ADD PRACTICAL VALUE

In 1986, Al Rappaport wrote *Creating Shareholder Value*. Five years later, Bennett Stewart wrote *The Quest for Value*. Both books took the principles of corporate finance and provided value-led organizations with a way of using those principles to change dramatically the way they managed their businesses. Their work is important in demonstrating how to take the techniques of valuation and cost of capital and apply them to understand value creation within the organization. While financial and management accounting addresses profit and loss statements, and corporate finance addresses net present value, the breakthrough here was development of economic profit or economic value measures of performance.

These works discussed not only how to calculate the amounts but how to apply the information. Until these breakthroughs, organizations did not have the methodologies to manage for value. With this information, organizations could begin to apply the methodologies.

In these and similar works, the applications discussed primarily included stock picking (for investors) and, for value-led organizations, the calculations and the applications to capital budgeting and compensation.

Because the information was new, the early works discussed theoretical applications and methodologies. Over the 1980s and 1990s, these approaches began to be customized and refined as value-led organizations adopted these practices. Compensation was one major area where this occurred. As the theory has evolved, value-led organizations have also evolved in their use of the new disciplines.

CORPORATE GOVERNANCE

There has also been an evolution in the area of corporate governance. Robert Monks and Nell Minow have written several important works (described in Chapter 9) that discuss the principles of good corporate governance and provide case studies and examples of their applications.

The use of value techniques by investment professionals is growing. Analyst firms have begun to use the techniques, as have pension and mutual fund managers. For example, Odey Asset Management Limited (discussed in Chapter 7), a UK investment firm, uses economic value calculations to help determine its investment choices.

In 1998, CALpers, the largest pension fund in the US, with $160 billion in assets under management in 2001, issued a statement that it would not only be using the metrics to assess companies, but would also invest in companies based on whether those companies used value-based principles in running and managing their business.

GM & GE AHEAD OF THE CURVE

Probably some of the earliest adopters of metrics and compensation were General Motors and General Electric. As early as the 1920s, GM established a compensation program that included a charge for the cost of capital. And, in the 1950s, GE adopted a simple version of the measure, called residual income. Residual income was calculated simply as net income less a charge for the cost of equity capital.

THE EVOLUTION: SHAREHOLDER RIGHTS AND COMPENSATION

The recognition that organizations should govern in a value-led manner has just grown since then. As more organizations become value-led, more is learned and the methodologies and approaches become more and more refined.

Along with this movement, there has also come an increase in shareholder rights awareness and reactions. Proxy voting has become an important part of the shareholder investment process. In addition, shareholders have begun to place an even greater emphasis on the governance processes of an organization. Today, many organizations include issues for proxy vote that have been submitted by individual shareholders or shareholder groups. These issues may include, for example, value stands on the environment, on supplier qualifications, on executive compensation or board compensation. This activism has caused value-led organizations to expand their awareness and clarify their values even further.

As the theories and awareness have evolved, so have value-led organizations evolved:

» from metrics alone to compensation to training to multi-constituent level thought processes;
» from simple to more refined uses and application of metrics, compensation, training, communications, and decision-making processes.

In the evolution of compensation practices, for example, value-led firms have evolved along several lines. One has been a gradual increase in the percentage of pay that is variable and performance driven. Another is the percentage of staff receiving variable pay packages. In the 1970s and earlier, most variable pay arrangements were primarily focused on top executives. During the 1980s and 1990s and into this century, value-led firms have expanded the use of variable pay plans. At first, this began by including middle management and then spread further throughout the organization. Briggs and Stratton, for example, even extended the process to include front-line union workers as well.

Compensation has also evolved as value-led organizations have sought to improve the linkage between behavior and performance measures. For example, stock grants or stock options might not make sense for everyone throughout the organization. Plans instead needed to be derived from value creation information, or drivers of value. These efforts began to refine the compensation mechanisms beyond those first articulated. In addition, the techniques for top executives were also improved.

Value-led organizations have had to seek new mechanisms because traditional compensation plans are not aligned with value creation. These plans can result in executives being paid lucrative bonuses even when no value has been created. Even using traditional stock plans can cause issues. For example, a manager might be highly rewarded if the share price has gone up, even if competitor stock prices have risen further. To be value-led, organizations have had to be willing to experiment. Value-led firms have been at the forefront of developing meaningful and challenging compensation programs. (This will be discussed further in Chapter 6.) The work continues to evolve and is critical to continuing the progress within value-led organizations. (See Fig. 3.1.)

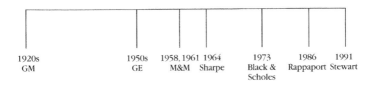

| 1920s | | 1950s | 1958, 1961 | 1964 | 1973 | 1986 | 1991 |
| GM | | GE | M&M | Sharpe | Black & Scholes | Rappaport | Stewart |

Fig. 3.1   Evolution of value concepts.

NOTES

1 Modigliani, F. and Miller, M. (June 1958) "The cost of capital, corporation finance, and the theory of investment," *American Economic Review*.
2 Modigliani, F. and Miller, M. (October 1961) "Dividend policy growth, and the valuation of shares," *Journal of Business*.
3 Sharpe, W. (September 1964) "Capital asset pricing in a theory of market equilibrium under conditions of risk," *The Journal of Finance*.
4 Black, F. and Scholes, M. (May–June 1973) "The pricing of options and corporate liabilities," *Journal of Political Economy*.

The E-Dimension of Value-led Organizations

» With the advent of the Internet, value-led organizations are faced with new issues and opportunities.
» Value-led organizations must carefully weigh all aspects of e-strategy implementation.
» The valuation and assessment of e-commerce benefits and costs is more complicated than many organizations realize.
» Value-led organizations use the availability of the new technology as an opportunity to address both old and new organizational problems.

The Internet and the World Wide Web have transformed the way businesses and their customers operate; they have also created new issues for value-led organizations.

One primary issue is the role that the web will play in an organization's strategy. Before any decision is taken on this role within an organization, the question of how the Internet influences individuals and firms should be considered on three dimensions:

» Information gathering
» Information distribution
» Transaction consummation.

Using these three dimensions, value-led organizations must determine which, if any, of their activities will use the Internet for these purposes. While this may seem relatively simple, the issue is more complicated than it might first appear. The cost of web development and maintenance can represent a sizeable initial and ongoing investment in time and money for the firm. The ethical issues surrounding the web are new as well. To be value-led in this regard, organizations must understand all of the impacts before embarking on web initiatives.

One of the first considerations is the fiduciary responsibility to the shareholder. The questions to be addressed include whether the use of the Internet (and its concomitant cost) will benefit the shareholder over the long term, and how best to use the Internet to maximize value. To answer these questions requires an organization to be able to apply calculations of economic value at a fairly sophisticated level. To do this well, the organization must estimate and calculate the impacts of many scenarios in order to understand which ones will maximize shareholder value. These scenarios would include the use of the Internet for multiple combinations and permutations of the three dimensions listed above. Once the possibilities have been outlined, the organization must make reasonable estimates of the cost of development for each scenario, and of its potential benefits. Because the Internet represents a new and different means of accomplishing the work of the firm, its costs and potential benefits cannot be viewed in isolation. In fact, value-led organizations must spend time considering and determining the follow-on effects of any given implementation. For example, these follow-on effects might include impacts on:

» other information gathering mechanisms,
» other distribution channels,
» the ability to cross-sell products and services,
» competition, the ability to compete and the nature of competition,
» staff,
» suppliers,
» customers,
» shareholders.

The scenario analyses based on the three dimensions will determine which of these impacts will be significant.

THE THREE DIMENSIONS IN MORE DETAIL

Information gathering

Web-based information-gathering scenarios include use of the web by employees to gather information useful to the organization. An issue value-led organizations must address includes trusting employees to use the web for the benefit of the organization. Some organizations monitor employee use of the web to ferret out activities which are not work-related, or even offensive. It is important for value-led organizations to think through their approach to this serious issue. To address the issue with wisdom, value-led organizations need to be reflective on the issues that might give rise to their concerns. For example, an organization could take this as an opportunity to address motivational issues of employees. In a reflective mode, the organization might wish to address to what degree management, for example, has acted with stewardship in relation to its employees and its shareholders. One question to address might be to what extent employees believe there is a value in spending their time on the company's initiatives. These questions go right to the heart of motivation and the questions raised by the presence of the Internet provide an opportunity for organizations to address them.

This opportunity also occurs related to the enormous potential provided by the Internet to gather more information than ever before. To reap the benefits, value-led organizations must make sure they are prepared to act on the new ideas and sources of information that are provided. They must ensure that mechanisms are instituted so that employees are encouraged to provide their ideas based on the new information.

In the US, for example, room for improvement apparently exists with or without the Internet. Citing an Employee Involvement Association study, Roxanne Emmerich says in an article entitled "The 10 commandments of workplace motivation," (*AirTran Arrivals*, June/July 2001) that "the average employee in Japan submits 32 ideas for improvement per year, compared to the average employee in the US who submits .17 – a ratio of 188 to 1."" The root of the problem," Emmerich goes on, "stems from the fact that only 33 percent of US employees' ideas are adopted, compared to 87 percent from Japanese workers."

Value-led organizations must have mechanisms that encourage improving the utility of the newly available Internet information. To do this effectively, they need mechanisms to:

» take the ideas,
» rapidly evaluate their value impact, and
» communicate their decisions on implementing new practices.

The Internet, of course, can be used as a tool to help organizations to do just that.

Web-based information-gathering scenarios may include new mechanisms for gathering information about prospects and customers. A website may provide the firm with an opportunity to gather new information from prospects and customers as part of the browsing experience or in return for value-added information. Value-led organizations must evaluate the long-term *versus* short-term impacts of the data gathering. They must determine what information to gather and how to gather it. Once it is gathered, value-led organizations must also determine its appropriate use. Issues to be determined include formulation of privacy policies related to the information disclosed, and the use of cookies to write information to users' personal computers and then gather that information during subsequent logins.

Another use of the Internet may be to provide a new means of gathering information from suppliers. Again, value-led organizations must weigh the impacts of these requirements. One issue often overlooked in this area is data quality. Organizations must weigh the true costs and benefits taking these issues into account.

Information distribution

Web-based information distribution scenarios may include providing information and proxy voting to shareholders via the web. Value-led organizations must consider the extent to which they will use the web to provide information to investors via the web as well. In line with its fiduciary responsibility, the web provides a relatively cheap and effective means of communicating information to shareholders. Value-led firms can not only provide standard annual and quarterly report information on-line, but also keep investors and others informed of their business activities, with frequent updates and reports. As investors continue to require more and more transparency, some firms are responding by providing more and more information in web-based format. In the US, regulation FD (fair disclosure) by the SEC requires publicly-traded companies to share material information with all investors simultaneously. Due to this requirement, many organizations are providing power-point slides for download from the web and web-casting meetings with analysts and institutional investors. This has provided more information to individual investors, which, undoubtedly, is a good thing for both parties.

The issue that value-led organizations must resolve, however, on all these fronts is access. Use of the web assumes universal access to this utility. For many investors, this may be true; but there continue be issues of access for others. According to an article by Sarah Smith entitled "Wired world" in *Psychology Today* (August 2001), it was estimated that approximately one third of US households at the time had personal computers. Making information available through a variety of formats, and not solely through the Internet, is an issue that value-led organizations should consider.

Information distribution may be developed for imparting information to customers. This may include product information available on the website. It may involve providing product and sales information by emails to customers and to prospects. In thinking about these scenarios, value-led companies must consider the extent to which information, from the customer's perspective, would be valued, and whether it can help the organization to:

» improve cross-sell;
» increase customer loyalty; and
» increase use of this distribution channel.

In terms of information gathering and distribution (i.e. communications), the Internet provides ways for value-led organizations to address their employees' concerns about the work/life balance, and community and environmental concerns related to carbon monoxide emissions. By using the Internet to reframe work operations, the potential exists to allow employees to be more productive, to eliminate the stress and pollution from commuting, and to reduce their personal and corporate expenses by working from home. Again, trust may become an issue. Value-led organizations that follow this path take the opportunity to address motivation issues and to find the right overall balance between email communications and in-person meetings to accomplish their tasks. Work styles of many employees and synergistic developments will often be better supported by balancing the approaches effectively. Value-led organizations must weigh these positive benefits against the potential downside risks.

In certain circumstances, organizations have had to take positive steps to address the use of email systems when they have caused issues in productivity. Email systems can become postponement and blame systems if the organization does not take action. Individuals have the ability to "pass the buck" vial email rather than address issues head on or face-to-face. To prevent email systems from becoming politically charged, value-led organizations take the opportunity to work consciously to create a culture focused on results, and to review practices that might exacerbate lack of co-operation within the organization. In some organizations, courtesy standards are set, as well as responsiveness standards. In addition, value-led organizations will examine reward structures so that email systems promote rather than reduce productivity.

Transaction consummation

A natural extension of information distribution is the use of the web for transaction consummation. Transaction consummation refers to the actual completion of transactions on-line. Primarily it refers to sales transactions between the customer and the organization, although it can refer to other transactions as well. In analyzing the impacts of the web for transactional purposes, value-led organizations must estimate the follow-on effects. Issues to review include cannibalism, market segmentation, and staffing. Cannibalism refers to the extent to which the Internet channel replaces other distribution channels. Market segmentation refers to understanding which customers might use which channels. And staffing refers to the ways in which the Internet might have an impact on the organization's human capital.

Early in the e-revolution, many organizations created two separate entities, web and non-web. These entities did not interact with one another and were managed separately, often with two different sets of staff. From a customer perspective, this often resulted in customer service problems. As value-led organizations consider the importance of integration from both the customer and employee perspective, structuring the integration properly is key to maximizing value.

Transaction consummation can raise privacy and security issues that value-led organizations must address and build into their business plan scenarios. Failure to recognize these potential costs can be a critical mistake in understanding the investment impacts. In addition to sales to customers, transaction consummation scenarios may also involve payment systems with suppliers as well. Value-led organizations will continue to consider carefully the value-added benefits of new Internet processes as software is increasingly deployed by ASPs (application service providers) on the Internet.

STRATEGY CONSIDERATIONS

Use of the Internet is truly a strategic decision with the capability of fundamentally changing an organization's business processes and business proposition. Value-led organizations must determine what is core and strategic for them and what they are willing to commoditize. (The Internet can be used to commoditize parts of their operation and it can also help to emphasize their unique value proposition.) In reviewing their strategic use of the web, value-led organizations must consider the impact on their competitive environment. These issues may include the impact of the Internet on:

» competition;
» the ability to compete; and
» the nature of competition.

Questions that organizations must answer include the level of information that they are willing to make freely accessible to the competition; the extent to which they want to be leaders or followers in web use; how their uses of the web will effect how they compete; and what strategies they can employ to use the web to create more value by changing the nature of the way in which they must now compete.

The web can create lower barriers of entry. With its advent, value-led organizations more than ever must understand the value they create, and then communicate it effectively.

BEST PRACTICE RESPECTS PRIVACY

With the technological advances of the Internet, the ability of organizations to gather information about their customers has increased. The issue of consumer privacy for financial institutions is regulated within the US, and financial services organizations have been obligated to send notices to customers allowing them to opt out of having their information shared. In many cases, the process that customers must follow to opt out has not been very user-friendly.

Although the issue is critical within financial services, it is also an important issue for all Internet organizations and their customers. One area, along with financial services, that represents one of the most-used consumer business transactions on the Internet is travel.

Travel sites are able to gather a great deal of information on those who browse and buy airline, hotel, car rental, and related services. These items often represent big-ticket items for households. In late 2000 and early 2001, there was considerable media debate about how travel sites gathered consumer information and how they used it to offer differential prices to different consumers for the same service. For example, the travel site might charge a first time buyer less to get them "hooked" on that site. It might raise rates on those who tend to browse and never buy. It might even review the last price paid (to determine the amount that the customer is willing to pay) and charge accordingly. In addition to the direct privacy concerns, these behaviors have heightened the focus on Internet privacy issues.

Privacy and the responsible use of customer information is a stewardship issue – a relationship issue for value-led firms. Recently, an example of good practice was cited in a US News and World Report article on the issue of privacy. In an article entitled "Gospel of privacy guru: Be wary; assume the worst," (Dana Hawkins, *US News and World Reports,* June 25, 2001) Larry Ponemon, "the ultimate privacy insider" named Expedia, a travel website, as a best practice example in the privacy arena. Ponemon explained: "There's an incredible amount of data in your travel profile . . . they improved security and created a sophisticated way to anonymize data . . . They spent millions because they understand their business strategy depends upon customer trust and loyalty." Ponemon, a privacy and technology consultant, contrasted these actions with those of many of his other clients who, for the most part, failed to take action or post the results of his privacy audits. "The invasions of privacy usually stemmed from ignorance," he states, "although in a few cases the companies were truly evil."

Value-led organizations take their responsibility as stewards seriously. They effectively balance issues of short-term profits and long-term value creation. They also consider the cost of "anonymizer" technology when implementing call-center or Internet sites. In the areas of health, finances, and habits of living, value-led organizations, like Expedia, do what is required to secure customer trust and confidence.

The Impact of Globalization on Value-led Organizations

» Assessment of culture is critical to successful implementation of global strategies.
» Value-led firms establish policies on a number of dimensions when entering foreign markets.
» Globalization complicates measurement issues and these issues must be addressed to ensure good decision making.
» Globalization has expanded the opportunities for value-led firms to benefit from multiple alliances and partnerships.

AN OVERVIEW OF THE MAJOR ISSUES

There are several implications of globalization that large value-led organizations must consider. In terms of the risks that a board must confront,
international risk is the largest. To address this risk, value-led organizations must ensure that board members and the executive management
understand global issues and global markets. Taking advantage of the
opportunities, while mitigating the risks, is key for the organization to
create value.

Even small organizations today must think globally in order to
compete successfully. To do this, they must successfully address a
number of value issues associated with globalization.

One key issue any organization must address is its ability to leverage
its operations by selling overseas. To do this effectively, the needs
of new markets must be assessed separately. The organization must
determine the true costs of product customization and estimate the
potential revenues and ongoing benefits provided to customers.

Another opportunity that globalization provides is the ability to
relocate operations to increase shareholder value. Here, value-led organizations must weigh political, economic and currency risks in other
locations. In addition, human rights issues and standards must be
addressed.

Today, while many shareholders care about bottom-line results, they
are also raising concerns about the responsibility the company has
to its employees. "Sweat shops" are not only distasteful, but create
tremendous reputation risk as well. While profitable in the short run,
such decision-making is recognized by value-led organizations as having
long-term negative effects on the company.

With the recognition that we are on one planet, globalization causes
value-led organizations to create operations in other countries that
create shareholder value without exploiting the people or environment abroad. Value-led companies establish standards and "high water
marks" to ensure that operations everywhere meet the value requirements. This can sound easier than it is.

VALUES, CULTURE, DIVERSITY, AND LANGUAGE

Globalization can have many impacts on a company from a value
management standpoint. The value systems in different locations may

be very different. While specifically confronted by organizations in offshore operations, increased globalization also affects workforce diversity at home. Value-led organizations systematically address these issues throughout the organization. Failure to understand them can cause significant issues in motivation, productivity, and outcomes. Written for a US audience in an increasingly global environment, the author's article "Performance through US binoculars" (*Journal of Strategic Performance Measurement*, October 1999) discusses the attributes that organizations must confront in order to address divergent values and develop mechanisms to enhance performance. To do this effectively, organizations must assess their cultures, and the perspectives and the world-views of the individuals that work in them.

To do this well, an organization must be willing to look deeply within itself. The manifestation of different cultures and values is often hidden, particularly within the hierarchal framework in which many old-style companies are run. To understand the cultures and motivations within the firm requires the value-led organization to look beneath the stated and ideal cultures (i.e. the organization's description of its culture and its statement of the ideal in terms of vision and values objectives) to the real culture and subcultures of the organization. Applying the law of physics ("for each action there is an equally powerful opposite reaction") means that an organization is wise to look at the undercurrents and the possible future impacts of cultural shifts (the evolving culture) and be prepared to handle them. A good starting-place for value-led firms is to review the multiple dimensions of attitudes within the organization that are related to when, who, how, and what.

Understanding attitudes helps an organization to understand individuals' intentions and the issues related to stewardship.

One area that must be addressed relates to *when*, or time. Attitudes about time can vary a great deal. For example, a description of attitude toward time might include the extent that:

» the focus is short-term or long-term;
» change or *status quo* is revered;
» fast or slow change is expected; and
» time is viewed as scarce or abundant, and scheduling structured or fluid.

Another area to consider is attitudes about *who*, or relationship. For example, how important is long history, to what extent is accountability viewed and problem solving expected at an individual or group level, how are individuals expected to work together – through fluid or structured relationships, and to what extent is collaboration *versus* confrontation valued.

In terms of *how* work is done, attitudes about process must be assessed. What are the values in terms of outcomes *versus* relationships, written or oral agreements, explicit or non-specific understandings, dispassionate or emotional communications, risk taking or avoidance, perfection or action, execution or planning?

And finally, how does the culture view success, *what* will it do from a decision-making perspective? Are the criteria for success achievement or affiliation, what is done (result) or how it was approached (process)? And what are the values associated with the decision-making: egalitarian or hierarchal, multiple views or one, consensus or mandate?

Once they have assessed these issues, value-led organizations must understand how to adapt and adopt their management objectives both to motivate and to challenge the multiple competing underlying views. Awareness is the first step.

On a practical level, these issues can affect how a company organizes or adapts certain processes. One area where this has been an issue is rewards and incentives. The structure of fixed *versus* variable pay, for example; ways of rewarding performance can be very different depending on the culture. Even within the same country, there may be a dichotomy in terms of how old-established firms attract and retain staff compared to newer start-ups. Value-led organizations not only understand current expectations of a culture, but also work proactively to improve and shape new dynamics within that culture. Have elements in the society been left behind? Can realignment provide advantages for potential employees and shareholders alike?

Certainly, even without offshore operations, globalization has created more diverse workforces and board memberships. This diversity, if managed well, can create competitive advantage and enhanced share-holder value as noted by the author in her article "Advantages of board diversity outweigh disadvantages" (*The National Association of Corporate Directors Monthly* May 2001). Value-led organizations will be more effective if multiple approaches are considered. Diversity provides the best opportunity to obtain multiple views.

To encourage these views, value-led organizations must recognize preconditioned tendencies that move against them and address these patterns. In this context, they must recognize the issue as more than a need to meet legal or social mandates. Rather they must provide an ongoing training commitment and make it a focus in every decision, problem-solving process, and product structure.

Value-led organizations recognize that diversity issues are not just "employee" related but that globalization has also impacted on who their customers and shareholders are. Globalization has created the need for executives and companies to be able to communicate with a variety of groups using alternative styles and means of expression. Different approaches will work more or less effectively in different settings. Executives must understand this in talking to employees and to the media. And the company must understand this when communicating the value proposition of its products to customers.

The role of CEO as spokesperson in a global economy has transformed the requirements of the job. CEOs must be culturally aware. Communications with the media in one setting may need to be modified for addressing individuals in other countries. Value-led organizations ensure that cultural awareness and standards are understood throughout the organization, not just at the board and CEO levels.

With the advent of the European Union, for example, US companies must be more aware of its potential effect on issues associated with European operations. In 2001, the EU, as part of its antitrust review, stopped GE's merger with Honeywell. Awareness of potential actions and their options value *must* be factored into global decisions related to markets and operations.

Globalization has also created the need for companies to address different languages as well as culture. This issue is covered in depth in ExpressExec's volume on *Managing Diversity* in this series. Value-led organizations anticipate the market benefits of product offerings and customer service operations able to handle multiple languages. Understanding market segments well becomes an even more important task for value-led organizations given the effects of globalization.

VALUE METRICS

To understand more fully whether, in fact, they are creating value around the globe, organizations must adopt more sophisticated measurement techniques, including economic value measurements which take into account, as required, different currencies and costs of capital.

From the standpoint of calculating and understanding economic value correctly, globalization has certainly complicated the work of boards and management. Globalization increases the company's need to slice and dice information along additional dimensions, by multiple geographies. Depending on the global opportunities value-led organizations have exercised, it may also mean additional new business areas as well. Treasury management is more complex with currency risks often handled both locally and centrally. In calculating economic value, these costs and risks must be considered.

Globalization may afford the organization the opportunity to raise funds in different locations. Value-led organizations will consider these issues in their decision-making.

Taking advantage of globalization allows value-led organizations to exercise the options value that global opportunities afford and to calculate these values in their estimates. One example of this is recognizing the brand recognition benefits of multi-operating and distribution locations. With more mobile business and pleasure travelers, worldwide brand recognition can have a positive multiplier effect. In the same way, working knowledge of operating in a particular country can be used by value-led organizations to become marketing arms for additional products and services. Value-led organizations recognize this potential options value.

OPPORTUNITIES AND RISKS

Globalization allows organizations to seek out other geographic operational opportunities. Organizations must choose whether a variety of locations make sense and, if so, whether to set up a new location run by the firm or to outsource the operations locally.

Value-led organizations recognize the need to seek out opportunities that most effectively exploit the core strengths of geography. Today, those core strengths may as often be human resources (training and intellectual capital) as natural resources.

Globalization causes value-led organizations to become even more diligent in their outsourcing practices. In outsourcing and location decisions, value-led organizations must consider not only cost benefits but risk issues as well. Just as at home, to mitigate risks, financial statements and corporate governance structures of suppliers and customers must be carefully assessed, particularly if long-term contracts are involved. Value-led organizations will want to scrutinize the boards of these organizations. For example, diverse boards can mean a stronger company. Some foreign entities may not have adopted these standards. Independence of the board can be another issue as well. And financial reporting standards may be more or less robust depending on the location. Because of this, value-led organizations may find:

» that profits on a like basis are quite different from the originally reported financial statement profits;
» a different level of discretion in reporting numbers; and
» a different economic value calculation due to differences in the cost of capital (in part attributable to lack of transparency and governance standards).

Political risk is a major issue in certain parts of the world and value-led organizations must find efficient ways to assess the risk and monitor it. Establishment of risk mitigation efforts is important. Just as lobbying efforts in the original country may be necessary and cost-justified, globalization can create the need in other locations as well.

Value-led organizations think through and are very clear on defining appropriate motivations and actions. And they draw careful lines on the continuum between persuasion and bribery. This careful analysis of the individual context of each situation is important in decision-making. Understanding the culture, as described earlier, can be very important in assessing the risks and the actions to mitigate those risks.

While globalization provides many opportunities for value-led organizations, it also increases the source of their competition. To address this effectively, value-led organizations focus on doing an even better job of strategic analyses. Specifically, they reflect seriously on their core competencies to ensure that *they* do what they know best, and hire the rest. They continually look to find new ways to create partnerships and alliances with firms overseas in ways that will add value to their own and to their partner's organizations.

A key issue that value-led organizations address in all these dimensions is intellectual capital, and where best to source it. By understanding the competitive landscape, value-led organizations make the adjustments necessary to compete effectively and to create motivated cultures. They also address the measurement and incentive issues in each context in a way that supports the values of the firm.

SOME EXAMPLES OF BEST PRACTICE

Globalization affects many organizations more than they recognize. The case of GE and Honeywell mentioned earlier in this chapter is just such an example: in this case, United Technologies understood the importance of globalization and was able to have a significant influence on the GE–Honeywell decision.

As reported in an article by Laurie P. Cohen in the *Wall Street Journal* on July 2, 2001 entitled "How United Technologies' lawyers outmaneuvered GE: their antitrust argument proved 'helpful' to Brussels Commission and caught rivals flat-footed," United Technologies found a way to make globalization work for them rather than against them. The first thing the article points out is that United Technologies demonstrated an understanding of subtle cultural influences. To meet its fiduciary responsibility to their shareholders, United Technologies needed to demonstrate that GE's proposed purchase of Honeywell represented an antitrust risk.

While others may have crafted the details of the argument, United Technologies instead carefully chose who would present to the regulators in Brussels. In this case, in Cohen's words, they picked "Janusz Ordover, a Polish-born economist, on the grounds that his attire and his accent would play better with regulators in Brussels. Even GE's own top economist on the deal believes that this grasp of such cultural nuances paid off: 'Janusz is a trans-Atlantic guy' says the GE antitrust economist."

In addition, United Technologies understood the need for speed, communication, and cultural sensitivity in its legal team. United Technologies used the same counsel in both the US and Brussels. This, in part, is credited to the company as being responsible for its ability to make a case that was persuasive. There may be arguments about other aspects of the situation and about what took place; however, United Technologies demonstrated the advantages of cultural sensitivity. This was, no doubt, an important factor in the result.

Three value-led organizations deserve kudos for helping organizations to understand the importance of globalization on corporate governance. They include the International Corporate Governance Network, Corporate Women Directors International, and the National Association of Corporate Directors. The latter two recently sponsored a "Colloquium for Women Corporate Directors: 'The 21st Century Corporate Board'." Much of the program of this colloquium was devoted to the impacts of globalization on corporate governance. Edith Weiner, a futurist, gave a talk in which she pointed out that nation state sovereignty is being degraded, that information no longer respects human boundaries, and that global corporations are establishing the new boundaries in an age when more and more people are becoming citizens of the world. At this meeting of members of boards, speakers discussed issues of intellectual property and patent protection, of global accounting issues, global competition for capital, currency risk, and the issues of diverse regulatory requirements. The efforts of the value-led organizations these speakers represented, and of the organizations putting on the colloquium, represent best practice in attempting to address the issues of globalization not merely in a day-to-day reactionary sense, but in a well-thought process that starts at the very top of the organization – with the board of directors.

Current and Evolving Issues for Value-led Organizations

- » There are a number of controversial topics and key issues for value-led organizations today.
- » Board composition and board size is an area of controversy.
- » Value-led organizations continue to be challenged to maximize value through diverse boards, workforces, and supplier participation.
- » Reward structures continue to evolve.
- » Value-led organizations use value-led metrics for compensation and are starting to consider more carefully the mix of fixed and variable pay.
- » Metrics are continuing to evolve with human capital and options issues at the forefront.
- » Investor pressures continue to push organizations to be value-led.
- » Value-led organizations are recognizing the need for and benefits of education in value-related topics.

» Value-led organizations understand the need to provide the platform where a changing workforce can prosper.

» There is much work to be done and value-led organizations are the ones that will take up and meet the challenge.

STARTING AT THE TOP: THE BOARD

One issue faced by value-led organizations today concerns corporate governance and the role of the board of directors. How the board should be constituted and who should sit on it is an evolving and controversial topic. For the past few decades, common wisdom said that a smaller board was more efficient, better run and able to make decisions more effectively.

In 2000, Dan Dalton and Catherine Daly of Indiana University did some pioneering research which showed that larger boards were, in fact, more effective then smaller ones. In an article called "The board and financial performance: bigger is better," (*Director's Monthly*, August 2000) they posited the reasons. Specifically, they cited the ability of larger boards to provide access to resources through the networks of additional board members, the potential for higher quality advice, the ability to balance CEO power, greater diversity and thus better decision-making, and the potential of the larger board as a training ground for staff and for succession planning.

In a follow-on article in 2001, entitled "Advantages of diverse boards outweigh disadvantages," (*Director's Monthly*, May 2001), the author discussed the link between better decisions and larger board size. Larger boards provide diversity of thought and can address complex questions from multiple perspectives. Boards that are not diverse are more easily blind to both risks and opportunities.

While the research is clear, members of some boards do not share this view. And large and diverse boards can, of course, be unwieldy. To address the issue, there are two recommendations.

The first recommendation is proper facilitation of larger board meetings. Many organizations have used facilitation techniques in other areas of the organization. Using outside facilitators or trained internal ones can ensure participation by all members and optimal flows and exchanges of information.

The advantage of small groups is that generally the best voice on any given subject will be heard. It is very important that large groups are trained to hear and respond to the lone voice and to take paths perhaps not originally envisioned.

Where these dynamics are not understood, large boards will be no more effective than small ones. All board members must feel encouraged to participate. Any board where one or two members dominate will be less effective, no matter what the size is. Skill training in conflict resolution can help to promote maximum constructive give and take at meetings. This kind of training at both the board and individual levels can be very effective. Value-led organizations with boards that have availed themselves of this kind of "self-awareness" have reaped benefits in terms of better meetings and better decision-making.

The second recommendation for large boards is to structure committee sessions to handle effectively the work best done in small groups, and to use the larger board for matters requiring more resources or broader bench strength. This thoughtful structuring maximizes the benefits that a large, diversified board can bring.

A larger board allows value-led organizations to structure committees with individuals from diverse backgrounds and to rotate committee assignments as may be desirable. As requirements continue to evolve and committee work on boards becomes even more important, a larger board provides a more appropriate level of energy to handle the number of topics that must be addressed.

Value-led organizations use large diverse board structures to maximum benefit and use these techniques to make them most effective. By participating as members of corporate governance organizations, they can avail themselves of the necessary training and structure their board work for maximum effectiveness. (See the best practices box at the end of Chapter 5.)

WORKFORCE DIVERSITY AND PARTICIPATION

As with the issue of board participation, larger participation within the organization itself is an ongoing issue for value-led organizations. Deloitte Touche recently engaged in a series of successful focused efforts to encourage a more diverse work force. Although many value-led organizations are working to improve the access they provide, access continues to be an issue for women and minorities.

Some value-led firms attempt to address the access issue through flexible work programs, through training and through women and minority supplier efforts. Value-led organizations use these programs not only to provide opportunities to diverse work groups but also to improve their bottom line. Disadvantaged groups given opportunity are often most appreciative. And value-led organizations have found their efforts particularly successful when the organization addresses cultural issues that might mitigate the benefits. In terms of suppliers, as well, organizations find women and minority firms are often more willing to provide extra customer service because they appreciate the opportunities afforded them. Obviously, attracting the best talent and creating a work environment that will attract them makes sense to the bottom line. The diversity of perspective can be a critical factor in helping solve complex business problems. This whole issue is covered in depth in ExpressExec's title *Managing Diversity* in this series.

REWARD STRUCTURES

One recent trend in value-led organizations is to evaluate what pay-for-performance really means. William M. Mercer, for example, released a study in May 2001 of 350 large companies. This showed that CEO compensation was increasing most in companies with the best stock performance and decreasing if the company's stock performed poorly. While compensation consultants cite a link, corporate advocates often question the clear relationship.

Much controversy attends compensation questions related to the form of variable pay. Not only is the relationship between pay and performance often unclear, the means to achieve it is under dispute it as well.

In the late 1990s, many compensation consultants touted stock options as the solution to alignment, i.e. aligning management, employee, and board interests with that of shareholder value. Currently this practice has become more controversial. The reason for the controversy has surrounded the questions of whether, and to what extent, compensation in stock makes sense. And if it does, then whether stock options are a good compensation alternative. While less often discussed, stock as an incentive is a question that value-led organizations must address. While stock may represent a means of aligning interests with shareholders, care must be taken to structure the programs so that there is alignment between the long-term interests of pension holders and the recipients of the stock.

Although consultants and organizations began the practice in the 1990s, Al Rappaport popularized the idea of indexed options as a solution to the accountability issue in his article "New thinking on how to link executive pay with performance," (*Harvard Business Review*, March–April 1999). Despite this, options are still under suspicion, as Richard Wagner discussed in "Overcoming stock-option addiction," in *Executive Talent*, Spring 2001. The dilution impacts of stock options raise issues as well. While there are some ways to structure option and stock grants to address the long-term issues, value-led firms have a way out of the maze that is simple and solves multiple problems at once. They use value metrics and value-based compensation programs to align employee, board and management incentives with shareholder value interests.

This solves multiple problems at once by allowing for more specific alignment in the case of employee and non-board, non-CEO management compensation. That is because value metrics can break down value creation into component segments that more nearly relate to the contributions of individual or small groups within the firm.

Given the advantages, one might expect widespread adoption of value metrics for compensation. The advantage of value metrics, ironically, is what has impeded their general adoption. They require such honesty about results, a higher level in fact than is required in stock index-based incentives. After all, the stock market can always be blamed (rather than the performance of the company) if share prices drop. A lack of true accountability is the result. In the mid to late 1990s, this was especially true in the US when certain stock prices rose despite the lack of real performance to support the increases.

As discussed in Chapter 5 on globalization, different cultures have very different attitudes to variable pay. In some cultures, variable pay represents a very small part of overall compensation. In others, corporate executives expect the majority of their pay to come in some variable form. In addition to issues surrounding variable pay, however, new ways of thinking about "all-in pay" are just now beginning to receive attention. The author's article "Rewarding executives who know the score," in *Executive Talent*, Summer 2001 notes that many executive compensation programs begin by looking at what other organizations are doing with pay first, and then shaping a pay practice around this.

Value-led organizations are beginning to take a different pay approach. (See the examples of Bank One and Halma in Chapter 7.) Here, pay is truly related to value creation. While traditional concepts base executive pay on what others in similar positions receive, today the ability to measure value creation allows value-led firms to create true accountability with value-based compensation.

ACCOUNTABILITY AND CHANGE

This accountability represents a huge change within the organization. The enormity of change is one of the current topics in any discussion of value-led organizations. Bill Mahoney covered this topic in a recent interview with the author in *Shareholder Value Magazine*. ("Heading into a sea of change," March–April 2001). The purpose of the interview was to discover why, despite logic to the contrary, the adoption of value-management techniques was happening so slowly. Rather than the complexity of metrics, the author argued that becoming a value-led organization represented an enormous change for an organization. The magnitude of the change and the impacts on decision-making were primary issues in creating blockages to becoming value-led. In fact the changes are often underestimated. These changes include:

» decisions made on a new basis;
» new information about what is working or not working;
» new awareness about the relationship between investment and return; and
» new organizational structures and mechanisms.

THE METRICS

Value metrics are another area of controversy and continue to be a subject of much debate. Many methodologies exist and there is no one standard. There are dollar value metrics and percentage value metrics. Both measures use a cost of capital benchmark in calculations and assessments. This cost of capital calculation is also controversial, with strong advocates of CAPM methodologies and other equally robust advocates of multi-factor arbitrage models or other methodologies.

Some investment managers, who use value metrics to evaluate companies for the purposes of purchasing their stock, may not know how to calculate, or may not actually themselves calculate, the value metrics. Instead they may rely on analysts or some other service for the calculated numbers. While these organizations are to be commended, the inability to self-calculate the numbers represents the current state of the knowledge of this subject and the further work to be done. Just as value-led organizations have recognized the need for this information, organizations at the forefront have recognized the need to learn how to calculate these numbers for themselves. For a process that is part art and part science, this means digging deeply into the potential approaches and selecting one that works well for the organization.

Because value-based metrics include all costs, operating units are not just judged on what they produce, but on what they produce depending on what they have been given or have used. Improvement in value is derived by using less or producing more. Because value management balances these tradeoffs in its metrics process, there are no arbitrary constraints on size. In fact, value-led firms need not arbitrarily limit the size or scope of their operations. Determining their scope and scale is based on future predictions of value creation. This idea, while straightforward, can be controversial depending on the mindset of the leadership in some companies who believe that capital is limited and that their resources are as well. Value-led organizations work towards an understanding of their optimal growth paths and establish flexible financing systems so that operations can reach the optimal size for value creation. (See the example of Halma in Chapter 7.)

One controversy related to value metrics is whether value metrics cause an organization automatically to shrink capital. Value metrics allow organizations to make proper tradeoffs between using less and producing more. One key issue in this tradeoff can be the proper use of the metrics. Value-led organizations understand that value metrics properly applied do not circumscribe the size of the firm except in the context of value creation. This is an important area of focus today as more firms begin to use value metrics in managing their business. While value metrics do not, as the critics claim, cause an organization to shrink capital, they can do just that if they are misapplied. Most commonly a metric is misapplied when it is used to answer a question that would be best answered by using a different metric. One common example is the use of a percentage value measure to imply a need to shrink one aspect of the business, while growth would, in fact, add more value in dollar terms. In this case, the percentage value measure has been misapplied.

Apart from the calculations, however, there is still controversy about whether or not the metrics add value. Much of this research has been promulgated by accounting academics who focus on the value of earnings versus value metrics. Such studies focus on the predictive value of the metrics (in predicting stock price, for example), in part because certain consultants have focused on that aspect. Value-led organizations, however, tend to focus on the behavioral aspects of the measures and their ability to clarify motivation and intent. (See the examples of Bank One and Halma in Chapter 7.)

HUMAN CAPITAL AND OPTIONS VALUES

Besides general metrics discussions, another key issue for value-led organizations is the evolving area called Human Capital Measurement. As firms become less natural resource intensive and depend more on human resources for their value creation, this is becoming an important topic for value-led organizations. Value-led organizations seek to use human capital metrics to provide information on the operation of their businesses. As a backdrop, the value of human capital can be understood at the total corporate level and through evaluations of market expectations for innovations and improvements, a rough measure of the estimated value of human capital.

Another level of understanding is at the project or decision-making level where the value of endeavors can be measured. Improvements in the use and capacity of human capital can be made. What is new is the growing acceptance of this possibility.

Value-led organizations are beginning to understand and develop information on the human capital implications of decisions. As they view their operations more holistically, they are including these analyses in an action-oriented way. Specifically, value-led organizations are quantifying the value of initiatives that improve the use or capacity of human capital; for example, the internal measurement of the efficacy of and value created by training programs. These efforts by value-led organizations not only make the programs more effective but also provide a financial justification for their existence and continuation. Value-led organizations that impose these disciplines find it easier to choose between various human capital initiatives and to maintain momentum for these activities.

Another newer area in the metrics arena is the use of options value analysis in decision making. Pioneered by Judy Lewant, CFO at Merck and Company, Incorporated for the R&D efforts of the pharmaceutical industry, this area has become a new discipline for many value-led organizations. Before adoption, many organizations used traditional means to quantify decisions. However, intuition about the decisions always presented alternative views that either could not be or were not quantified. Using options value techniques, value-led organizations are able not only to quantify the overall impact of a variety of decisions, but also the best timing for the actions. (Timing, in particular, was often considered a qualitative rather than a quantitative decision.)

Using options value techniques, value-led organizations can quantify the options value of proceeding with a decision. This options value may include, for example, the opportunity value of follow-on decisions. A case might, for example, occur if an organization enters a certain market or develops a certain product. There may then be value that exists to extend the product line or market base as a result. This additional follow-on value is one potential options value of the decision. In other situations, there may be more options value in waiting or holding off on a particular decision. Waiting may provide a better opportunity in terms of strategic entry, of developing better alliances, or of enhancing product structure. The options value of waiting can also be quantified. Martha Amram and Nalin Kulatilaka discuss the use of options valuation in depth in their book, *Real Options: Managing Strategic Investment in an Uncertain World* (Harvard Business School Press, 1999).

As discussed in Chapter 5 on globalization, value-led organizations must factor in options value as it relates to foreign operations. The emergence of the European Union is beginning to change the competitive environment in Europe. Value-led organizations must be aware of the options value of proceeding or waiting. Proceeding may provide follow-on benefits; waiting may provide the value of better formulating strategy and avoiding reversals once certain political and economic frameworks have been determined. Such analyses can be very important to value-led organizations. Likewise, as discussed in Chapter 4, options value must also be considered in the context of the Internet: the options value of capturing first users in a particular area *versus* the options value of waiting and moving stealthily, at the right moment. In all these cases, options valuation techniques can be and are useful.

In an article entitled "Intangibles, human capital and options value measurement" published in the *Journal of Cost Management* in November 2000, the author provides an overview of options value in conjunction with human capital measurement. This extends the work in human capital measurement to include options valuation, a significant new area of exploration. For example, value-led organizations want to understand not only the immediate benefit of a training initiative, but also its options value.

ASSESSMENTS BY INVESTORS

Another key issue for value-led organizations is the area of shareholders' rights and good corporate governance. Over the last few years, value-led firms have been rewarded for their efforts by increased attention from larger pension plan sponsors. In the US, Calpers, which manages $160 billion, also considers corporate governance issues very strongly in its investment process.

In a discussion on value management, Roger Ford, former managing director of Prudential Investment Advisors, said to the author, "We want to know when a company is on the cusp of implementation. Then we know that the potential exists for a significant boost in stock price."

EDUCATION

Along with appropriate processes, there is an increasing focus by value-led organizations on cultural changes, on training, and new authority systems. One area that has again received recent press comment is open-book management. Coined in the early 1990s, the term refers to the sharing of financial information with and providing financial education to employees. The purpose of open-book management is to help employees to understand better the company's profitability dynamics. Armed with this knowledge, employees are better positioned to help the organization to achieve its aims.

Value-led organizations take this concept one step further. A key issue of focus for them today is financial education focused on value metrics and value drivers. (See the example of Bank One in Chapter 7.) Value drivers are metrics that relate to individuals and their work within the organization. These might include statistics such as number of calls handled per hour or number of customer inquiries resolved to satisfaction. These value drivers tie back directly to the organization's value creation. Today, value-led organizations are focusing not only on understanding value at the board and executive level, but driving that process through the organization. Education is a big piece of this process. This new emphasis also relates to the increasing focus on human capital measurements discussed earlier. As the benefits of applying these processes becomes more evident, more and more value-led organizations are adopting these practices. This movement is important because it is increasing both organizational effectiveness and the individual's intellectual capital as well. Doing a "both and" on organizational and individual benefits brings advantages to both, but it does run counter to command and control, and to fear-based management. As value-led organizations choose this journey, they reinforce the culture that they aspire to.

THE PEOPLE EQUATION

Value-led organizations understand that these educational issues go to the heart of motivation. As discussed in Chapter 4 on the Internet, value-led organizations are focused on getting the best out of their human capital resources, and this means focusing on what motivates employees.

While typical motivation theory talks about carrots and sticks, a number of factors affect the motivations of the current workforce. These include:

» more women working in executive positions or running businesses;
» two-career households;
» increased demand for skill-based human capital and supply issues in terms of meeting that demand;

» greater variability over time in the skills demanded (prompted in large measure by the growth of technology and explosion of information);
» demographic changes, including the fact that the majority of workers have never lived through a Great Depression; and
» greater political freedoms world wide.

All these factors working together have caused fear as a motivator to decrease.

Value-led organizations understand these shifts. By increasing the education in value concepts and in the organization overall, these organizations seize the opportunity to align the workforce more effectively and to increase the motivation as a consequence.

As discussed in Chapter 4 and Chapter 5, value-led organizations are establishing more open cultures. With proper information access, employees can create value from any position. Organizations that fail to harness this power create a big dilemma for themselves and for the individuals within them. Books have been published recently on the disillusionment of the twenty-somethings. When employees feel that their potentials are not being realised as they had expected, they seem to experience more disappointment, stress, and depression than past generations, who may have expected work to be boring and unfulfilling. The workforce, more than ever, is operating at or near the top of Maslow's hierarchy of needs.

Value-led organizations look to these changes and use the value of the metrics to change the relationship between the individual and the organization. Value metrics provide an accountability mechanism not possible otherwise. This accountability mechanism allows organizations to hand off roles and responsibilities and do arms-length monitoring. It allows organizations to do more by focusing action at the proper level, and by providing the supports required to have a culture that is open to change and to new information.

THE FUTURE

What is next for value-led organizations? Continuing to harness the power of what they know. Extending these processes throughout their organizations so that it is pervasive and long-lasting. Moving the processes outside the organization into their other relationships, into their alliances. Using the information to improve the dismal failure of most mergers to increase value. And using it not only to understand themselves better, but also their partners, their competitors, their customers, their environment, and their communities.

This is really the next frontier. Like financial education, soon value education will be mandatory. Value-led organizations will continue to reap the rewards of long-term integrative thinking – thinking open to change and open to a variety of sources for resolution of the problems that they and all those they come in contact with are trying to solve.

Value-led Organizations in Practice

Being value-led depends on leadership, but can only be successful if it is embraced by every single employee in an organization. The stimulus, and the decision which follows it, will be different, and will come at a different time, provoke a different response, and last for a different period, in every company. This chapter looks at the ways in which a number of value-led companies have responded to that challenge, exploring the examples of ten organizations, including:

» Prudential Insurance;
» Kmart;
» Bank One;
» Honda;
» Halma.

Being value-led depends on leadership. Ways of thinking and choices in each moment define what it means to be a value-led organization. Being value-led is not about turning a switch and everything is happily ever after. This is why, as discussed in Chapter 2, the extent to which an organization is value-led – in how many dimensions and in what time periods – changes and evolves. New managers may kick over the sand castles and build in their own ways. A leader who understands and articulates the value-based principles may be able to institutionalize them, at least for a time.

Some examples of value-led organizations are discussed in other resources. Briggs and Stratton Corporation is an example that is very well covered in two books: one by Al Ehrbar (*EVA: The Real Key to Creating Wealth*, 1998 John Wiley & Sons, Inc., New York) and the other by Joel Stern and John Shiely (*The EVA Challenge: Implementing Value Added Change in an Organization*, 2001 John Wiley & Sons, Inc., New York). The leadership team at Briggs and Stratton deserves kudos for the will of its leadership not only in implementing value creation principles but also in working to create sustainability and pervasiveness in their application.

Success stories differ in the way they come to pass. Often it is a challenge that sparks a leadership response. In those moments, it is the individual choice of organizations that causes them to be value-led. This chapter will discuss case studies of just those moments and of the organization that made those choices. The purpose is to show a number of ways that organizations can be and are value-led.

PRUDENTIAL(US): SEIZING THE OPPORTUNITY

The Prudential Insurance Company of America is an interesting example because it was not yet a stock-owned company when all this began. In fact, to put the story in context, it really began in the 1980s when Prudential purchased what was to become Prudential Securities from Bache Halsey Stuart. The firm was composed of a mutual fund operation (that made money), a brokerage arm and a middle market investment banking firm. There had been profit troubles and scandals throughout the 1980s and 1990s which had damaged morale throughout the company. There had been many attempts to deal with the problem, but nothing had succeeded in dealing with the fundamental issues. In addition to a spin-off of Prudential Securities scheduled for the fall of 2001, Prudential decided to take an even bolder (and value-led) move. As Brian O'Keefe wrote for *Fortune* magazine: "How do you restore integrity to Wall Street research – and make money too? Prudential has an answer." ("Rebuilding the rock," June 11, 2001.) Prudential's answer in 2001 was to reduce its investment banking operations significantly (by 80%) which, by this time, had less than a 1% share of market operations, and to refocus energies and attention on, as O'Keefe states "research – unbiased, uncompromised 100% investor-friendly research."

The impact of such a move is multidimensional. One aspect is Prudential's new ability to earn a decent return for its new shareholders. With US investors suffering significant losses beginning in early 2000, and the number of wealthy investors growing, more investors are looking for the kind of research and advice that will help them make better stock selection decisions. In this respect, Charles Schwab and Co. has embarked on a remarkable strategy to tier its client base and to develop more hands-on advice and resources to meet the growing challenge and demand of customer needs. From this perspective, the shift by Prudential uses customer needs to drive shareholder value. The value would come from increased trade volume directed to the brokerage operations of Prudential Securities. (This would be used to offset the loss of underwriting fees from investment banking.) More than that, however, it takes advantage of its own adversity to take a bold step forward in an area that will encourage other analyst organizations to be value-led. By providing "unbiased, uncompromised, 100% investor-friendly research," Prudential is helping to reshape an industry, much under fire now, that has unfortunately too often produced biased, investment banking client friendly research, i.e. research reluctant to take managements to task or provide the insight that investors need.

While it is easy to blame analysts, the issue is more widespread than that. Although institutional investors want to get the real scoop, they are not always anxious to search out bad news on companies they have already invested in. This can be witnessed in the questions they ask of corporate managements during analyst meetings. The questions are often routine and overly polite. No analyst or institutional investor wants to lose access to top management – for research and for ego reasons. Recently in the US, Regulation FD has created less ability for this access to provide benefits for research reasons (although the ego reasons still remain). In changing its model, Prudential is also helping to forge a new alternative for investors. In a press release on May 24, 2001, Michael J. Shea, president of the Equity Group of Prudential Securities said: "We are streamlining our stock ratings system and making plain our criteria. This rating change underscores our commitment to offering investors clear, credible research." As a result, "Prudential now lists 7% of the stocks it covers as sells – compared with an average of less than 1% at other firms." (Bill Mahoney, "Defining shareholder value," *Shareholder Value Magazine*, October–November 2000.)

PRUDENTIAL – KEY INSIGHTS

» Took the opportunity in its troubled investment banking unit to meet a growing customer need of unbiased research.
» Their response has the potential to help shareholders and change the nature of Wall Street research.

KMART: A TURNAROUND

Shareholder Value Magazine can be a great source of information on value-led organizations – organizations that are not in it for the short-term but, Bill Mahoney, the executive editor, notes "create value by servicing customers, improving productivity and optimizing alliances." Recently profiled in the magazine was Kmart Corporation. Kmart is an example of a US retailer that has suffered stiff competition in recent years. One of its chief competitors, profiled in Tom Peters' *In Search of Excellence*, is Wal-mart Stores, Inc., a value-led organization in driving cost efficiencies and staying attuned to what its customers want. In the May–June 2001 edition, *Shareholder Value Magazine* began coverage on Kmart and the new actions it is taking to build shareholder value and become value-led. One of the first things Chuck Conway noticed when he came on board as Kmart's CEO was that "profit is assessed without sufficient regard for the capital invested ... [also] we have complete disregard for the customer." Kmart has started a turnaround. This turnaround includes new performance metrics that take capital into consideration and customer satisfaction measures that really measure impacts on the customer. As a result of this focus on the customer, service levels on incoming 800 (toll-free) calls in the first 200 days moved from:

» 80% abandoned calls to 3%;
» average customer wait time of 10 minutes to less than 2 $1/2$ minutes;
» line availability of 30 hours per week to 24 hours per day.

Chuck Conway wrote, "The first signs of success are coming through. We led the retail industry at Christmas [2000]. . . our December comparable sales beat Wal-mart's. . . [we] ended the year with our first increase in market share in over 10 years!"

KMART – KEY INSIGHTS

» Is changing its business model by focusing on the customer and the shareholder.
» Is witnessing the results in increased sales and market share.

PFIZER, PROGRESSIVE, BERKSHIRE HATHAWAY, AND TREDEGAR: A TALE OF FOUR DISCLOSERS

"Information nourishes investors," says John Olson, a leading energy analyst (L. J. Rittenhouse, "Constructing change" *Shareholder Value Magazine* January–February 2001). Value-led organizations understand the benefits of full disclosures and transparency. One firm began complying with the US's Regulation FD (Fair Disclosure Rule), even before it was proposed. Pfizer, Inc.'s intention is to provide investors – big and small – with information about where it has been and what its strategies are. The goal is to provide more than the standard earnings release information. Several years ago, this process began to include 30 to 40 questions and answers that provided background information on the company and additional data to address the issues investors might have about the competitive environment and about Pfizer's future direction. (David Beck, "The secret's out: how to respond to Regulation FD," *Shareholder Value Magazine*, January–February 2001.) In this regard as well as in its board of governance, where it excels, Pfizer exhibits its value leadership.

> ## PFIZER – KEY INSIGHTS
> » Has strong board governance.
> » Provides investors – both big and small – with the information they want to know.

Progressive Casualty Insurance Company is a firm that, prior to Regulation FD, provided very little information to investors about its business plans. "In one of the boldest moves of the post Regulation FD era," beginning May 2001, Progressive is providing more information than it ever has to Wall Street and the general investing public and on a more frequent basis. As a result of Regulation FD, Tom Forrester, the chief financial officer of Progressive says "You had two responses to FD: either stonewall or open up ... it was clearly an opportunity for us to open up more." ("After Regulation FD, Progressive sets bold move," *Wall Street Journal* May 11, 2001 page C1.) Since the decision, Progressive reveals "premium volumes and ratios of underwriting profitability among other details of its operation" and it is not waiting for quarterly results. It is providing the information on a monthly basis. Progressive's move is significant because like Prudential's move to no-nonsense analysis it serves not only to benefit the investors of Progressive, but also to provide an example of a company that took the opportunity and made the choice to be value-led.

> ## PROGRESSIVE – KEY INSIGHTS
> » Took the opportunity of Regulation FD to provide more information to investors.
> » Represents a clear example of a company taking the opportunity and making the choice to be value-led.

Berkshire Hathaway Inc., the company in which Warren Buffet owns a sizable share, has always aimed to provide the information investors need, and in enough detail so that it can be properly evaluated by investors. In his annual reports, Buffet not only openly discusses what has occurred, both good and bad, but also the mistakes he has made and the opportunities missed. In his 1986 annual report, for example, he explained his philosophy this way: "The CEO who misleads others in public may eventually mislead himself in private." (Robert G. Hagstrom, Jr., 1995 *The Warren Buffet Way* John H. Wiley & Sons, New York.)

BERKSHIRE HATHAWAY – KEY INSIGHTS

» Has always openly discussed its mistakes and shared what has happened – good or bad – with investors.

» "The CEO who misleads others in public may eventually mislead himself in private."

Tredegar Corporation is a mid-sized producer of plastic films and aluminum extrusions. It also operates a small division in the medical technology business that has molecular compound, drug discovery and drug delivery operations. To help analysts and investors to understand it better, Tredegar uses its annual report not only to discuss the company and its future direction, but also to provide tools to help investors to use the information it provides to value the company their own way. The tools include metrics for each business and work sheets to help investors make their own valuation calculations. Not only is the company using its report to provide greater transparency, it is also, says Ed Cunningham, director of investor relations, "sending a message that we care about shareholder value." (Bill Mahoney, "Giving investors the valuations tools," *Shareholder Value Magazine*, January–February 2001.)

TREDEGAR – KEY INSIGHTS

» Has a complicated business and provides tools to help investors value its businesses.
» Sees disclosure as "sending a message that we care about shareholder value."

ODEY ASSET MANAGEMENT: USING VALUE TWO WAYS

Located in the attractive Mayfair area of London, Odey Asset Management, founded in 1991, currently manages hedge funds with three primary focuses: Europe, Japan and global. As with other value-led firms, certain distinguishing characteristics are readily apparent. For one, the members of the team, beginning with Crispin Odey, exude confidence without a trace of arrogance. Another characteristic, undoubtedly related to the first, is that they stand ready to admit mistakes or change approaches as needed. When in the business of buying, selling and short selling equities, this makes for a winning combination.

Crispin Odey, the firm's founder, explains his company's investment philosophy: "At the end of the year we must judge ourselves on the value, not the 'quality', of our portfolio. We feel that we are paid to change our minds, when appropriate. U-turns *are* allowed. Previous positions, convictions, philosophies, presentations and debates, where necessary, must be thrust aside by what is right now." (Dervia Keating, An interview with Crispin Odey of Odey Asset Management, Transparent Hedge Funds.com (www.transparenthedgefunds.com).)

Odey Asset Management exercises this philosophy by selecting stocks to buy or sell, then monitoring their movements in order to optimize the timing of the transactions. Rather than rely on the research supplied by Wall Street analysts, Odey utilizes its own in-house team that uses value-based metrics as part of its criteria. Using liquidity guidelines and stop losses, Odey's analysts actively control risk in their trading process. Odey estimates the cost of its risk controls to be about 5% of trading costs due to brokerage commissions. Its attitude toward risk controls is one of continual learning and improvement in its methodologies.

The most important performance measures used by Odey's employees to judge their own performance are value-based measures that consider the risk *versus* reward trade-off. They seek excellent returns with low betas and, unlike many portfolio managers, focus on high Sharpe and Sortino ratios for their portfolios. The Sharpe and Sortino ratios include measures of both risk and reward. (Beta, and the Sharpe and Sortino ratios are defined and described in the glossary in Chapter 8.)

Odey monitors its investments on a continual basis and when its technical signals indicate that it is time to buy or sell, it does so. This discipline has helped to minimize losses and Odey continually works towards sustained improvement of its stochastic and other technical models.

Like most value-led organizations, Odey's managers are solidly aligned with the results it produces. Crispin Odey has $30 million (approximately 70% of his liquid net worth) invested in the Odey European Fund. In fact, all of Odey's partners invest the majority of their net worth in the Odey funds. It creates a focus on value creation that benefits everyone.

ODEY ASSET MANAGEMENT – KEY INSIGHTS

» Confidence, not arrogance.
» Admit mistakes, change approaches as needed.
» Disciplined approaches under continuing review and improvement.
» Use value metrics to analyze potential investments and judge their internal performance.

BANK ONE: A TIME OF CHANGE AND A VISIONARY CEO

In 1995, Bank One Corporation embarked on a historic process of implementing value based management. Several factors came together to create a desire to move in this direction. One influence came from Fred Stratton, Chairman of Briggs and Stratton Corporation who is on the Board of Directors of Bank One. Briggs and Stratton had already gone through a similar process and Stratton encouraged John McCoy, CEO of Bank One, to take a look at the possibility. In 1995, the author developed value metrics that would provide greater explanatory power and presented them along with a recommendation that the metrics be implemented. Other individuals in the organization also presented similar ideas to McCoy during this same time period. McCoy had recognized the need to dismantle the Bank's "uncommon partnership." The uncommon partnership, a hallmark of McCoy's acquisition strategy, allowed newly-acquired banks to manage somewhat autonomously within a general framework and a strong performance measurement system. The reasons for the dismantling were many. One primary reason was the desire to improve the bank's ability to manage products across its retail system and to achieve cost savings through reduction in multiple overheads. As Roberto C. Goizueta, former Chairman of Coca-Cola, had realized, McCoy recognized that value metrics could become a rallying cry that would help the organization move through this immense change and undertaking. For strategic reasons, linking the two made sense.

In a discussion with the author, McCoy states "We were going to manage our businesses differently. Measurements are very important. We needed to refocus the way managers looked at the business." McCoy decided to move forward in 1995 and the implementation process for the first major bank in the US began.

By 1996, a project team was formed. At first progress was slow. Although banks had regulatory capital, banks were relatively new to the concepts of determining economic or risk capital. The bank organization was still in transition and, because of its historically decentralized structure, creating a change in culture of this magnitude was a tremendous undertaking. Because the new organization structure was not yet in place, line-of-business reporting information was not available.

Because of the size of the company and the undertaking, units were selected as "pilots" to begin to roll out the process. These pilots included units still on the old organizational structure and units that had already effectively undergone transition, or nearly so. The first step for the organization was education – a rallying cry for a better way to run the business.

While many organizations begin with a set of metrics, the Bank One culture had always operated on a consensus basis, a legacy, in part, of the uncommon partnership. To "buy in" to value-based management required a great deal of education in multiple forms.

To carry out this education, a variety of materials were developed. These included material used in meetings of small groups of 10 to 20 executives, managers, or staff; large presentations to groups of fifty or more; and small working groups of three to five people. Because of the geographic breadth, the core project team traveled to major sites throughout the US to explain the principles and the benefits of the new way of running the business. Articles were written for the monthly company newsletter. Flyers were developed and mailed answering FAQs (frequently asked questions). McCoy taped a video segment discussing the pilot work and the reasons for the change and the video was viewed by every employee throughout the company.

Ironically, Bank One's previous successes with measurement systems created some unique challenges for the training process. Several years before, Bank One's management reporting system had been showcased as state of the art and a model of accountability in *Harvard Business Review*. This management reporting system was a reflection of McCoy's belief in the importance of measures for management.

Dismantling the uncommon partnership and implementing value-based management meant dismantling and replacing the old management reporting system. Understanding the need for change was a particular challenge for those who had grown up in the smaller banks that had been combined to form Bank One. While each may have had its own views – together they were linked by pride in the past traditions.

For some in the finance group, it was a particular challenge because, at Bank One (as in many banks), finance was primarily composed of accountants rather than economists. For those individuals, tangible proof was more important than theoretical soundness. Tangible "proof," however, was difficult to provide because, although two smaller banks had implemented the value management process, no large or mid-size banks had attempted it. Where was the experience to back up the theory?

The change did indeed represent a switch from Bank One's traditional measures, but it made absolute sense given the change in Bank One's business model. Previously, Bank One had used ROA (return on assets) and had one of the best ROAs of all US banks. Now it was moving to less asset (i.e. loan) intensive businesses including investment management, brokerage, and insurance. It needed a measure that it could use across the board that would fairly assess the relative contribution of each operating unit. While the new metrics made sense to those in operations, some of the finance staff preferred the percentage measures of ROA or ROE (return on equity) that they were accustomed to using.

One of the seldom-discussed aspects of value implementation that was evident in this case was the ability of the process itself to transform the way individuals were thinking about their businesses. Through case examples in educational sessions, the impact of stewardship of capital was becoming understood. The discussions and the process gave managers a chance to step back and take a new look. This new look inspired changes in operations and in strategy.

In 1996, considerable progress was made in education and in developing metrics. In that year, a strategic planning process was instituted for the first time in the company's history. Along with this planning process came a rollout of the new metrics for planning purposes. McCoy spent time rallying the troops. It was the first time line-of-business numbers and plans were developed. The process worked very well.

In 1997, the work was extended beyond metrics and, with McCoy's support, work began on rollout of compensation plans using value-based metrics to the pilot units. With the link to compensation slated for the following year, the operating units began to focus even more strongly on the process. This focus included additional education and in-depth discussions on what the changes meant and how it would change the way the businesses were run.

To develop the plans, competitive information was gathered. Market and investor expectations and industry trends were identified. Many different analytical techniques were employed and shared with those involved in the implementation. The process was one of discovery for both operations management and the project team. What made the implementation so splendid was the awakening within the operations pilots and a growing understanding of the new insights and the dramatic changes in their way of doing business.

In 1997, after reviews of potential scenarios and the implications for the business areas, McCoy approved the pilot compensation plans. The plans had been carefully constructed. For management teams, there was both unlimited downside risk and upside potential. And the plans were constructed with clear insights into market expectations and the long-term view. Results under the new plans were not prone to manipulation. The plans included clear accountability for value creation and no bonus payments without the required results. Alignment had been established. They reflected clear stewardship and a new way of doing business. One of the units implemented a value-based plan for sales staff. Even this unit reaped tremendous benefits in more sales – more profitable sales and more value-creating sales.

McCoy was truly a visionary in recognizing the potential of this new way of looking at businesses, particularly in running a large financial institution. Even five years later, using these metrics at an operations level is still new to many financial institutions and using value-based metrics for compensation is even more leading edge. In July 2001, Morgan Stanley Dean Witter, a leader in this regard, has embarked on using these kinds of measures and processes for understanding the financial services industry and what is happening in specific organizations within that industry. For large financial institutions today, there is much yet to be learned by studying Bank One's historic process.

BANK ONE – KEY INSIGHTS

» A time of change.
» A visionary leader.
» Value management as a rallying cry to help the organization move through change.
» Education as the first step.
» Pilots as a way to rollout value metrics and compensation.
» Compensation with clear accountability.

HONDA: CONCERN FOR THE ENVIRONMENT

Honda Motor Co. Ltd is a company focused on creating products that provide value for customers. In that regard, "Honda's general policy, reiterated in the Annual Report 2000, is to allocate approximately 5% of its consolidated revenue toward R&D spending each year."

In 2000, this spending was even higher, in part because of the enhancement of environment-related technologies. Hiroyuki Yoshino, president and CEO of Honda wrote in a company brochure entitled "Can a company that makes cars meet the needs of its customers and the environment, too?,"

> "Exceeding the expectations of our customers while minimizing the impact our products have on the environment is part of Honda's guiding principles. Our responsibility and our commitment are to succeed at both challenges."

Honda focuses its environmental agenda in two ways. The more recent innovations are in developing products that can run alternative fuels. The other, which has been longstanding, is reducing emissions and increasing fuel efficiency. Honda's progress in this regard is demonstrated in its history over the last 25 to 30 years. Examples include the fact that in 1977 a Honda car was ranked first in fuel efficiency by the EPA (US environmental protection agency). In 1995, four Honda cars captured a spot on the EPA's top ten in fuel efficiency. In 1995, Honda made the first car to meet California's low emission standards and in 1997 to meet their ultra low emission standards. Honda's commitment has been longstanding and each year new advancements are made; from electric vehicles with advanced battery technology to new clean engine designs that beat previous years' records.

Honda's capital expenditures in 2001 and beyond are focused on meeting customer needs and continuing to preserve the value of the environment. This commitment is very explicit in the annual report. These expenditures focus on higher fuel efficiencies, lower emissions, quieter vehicles, and enhanced passenger safety. In addition, Honda is working to reduce the pollution from its manufacturing sites, a concept it calls the "green factory." Its efforts related to recycling and reuse are effective: the 2000 Annual Report says that "in 1999, the Susuka factory in Japan achieved zero level waste and the company is on course to realize its goal of zero waste at all factories in 2001."

As a value-led organization, Honda focuses its efforts on customer and environmental concerns.

HONDA – KEY INSIGHTS

» A focus on customers.
» A focus on R&D.
» A focus on the environment.

HALMA: SUSTAINABLE VALUE LEADERSHIP

Halma plc is indeed a value-led organization. With its headquarters in the UK and with businesses throughout the world, the organization focuses on generating shareholder value. Halma makes and markets products that are used to enhance safety and minimize hazards throughout the world.

"Most products either provide a warning of danger by detecting a hazard to life or health or ... protect against a particular risk ... World wide, there is a growing need for these products. The management teams create a flow of new products, continually enhancing the safety of users ... [For example,] every country needs more pure water for its population. Companies within the Group measure water contamination, sterilise water and produce equipment that stops clean water being lost from distribution networks ... Each company is expert at its own niche applications ... These are specialist businesses selling to skilled professionals who both demand and recognise optimum technical solutions. They also recognise the economic, social and environmental value of protecting their people and their assets."

Halma plc Website, www.halma.com/company/co_about.html
2001

Halma is value-led in a number of dimensions. In a company overview published on its website, it lays out its value-creation strategy:

''Our over-riding objective is to create shareholder value by

» building global businesses that sustain a leading position in specialised markets;
» concentrating on high-margin activities where products and services are differentiated on the basis of performance, not price, and where barriers to entry are high;
» tightly managing our asset base in order to maintain our outstanding operating ratios and powerful cash generation;
» investing in marketing, new product development and innovation to maintain high organic growth;
» acquiring businesses and intellectual assets that extend our existing activities, add value and will produce our exceptional operating ratios;
» maintaining a high return on capital employed to self-fund organic growth, acquisition activity and rising dividends;
» recruiting and retaining top quality management by preserving an entrepreneurial culture within a framework of rigorous financial planning, reporting, and control.''

In an interview with the author, Stephen O'Shea, chief executive, explains it this way: ''The essence of it is that we recognize that we are owned by our current shareholders. They have already bought our shares. And those shareholders include ourselves, the employees of the firm. Many of us have large stakes in the business, so we are both employees and shareholders.

''We understand we are there for the shareholder. We identify ways that will contribute to our long-term success, not fashions of the moment. We generate very powerful free cash flow every year. We are not constrained as others might be. We are self-reliant and focus on doing the right thing. This works on the basis of intellectual assets, more than physical ones. We create and sell unique intellectual products over and over to different markets and create market dominance with our intellectual property.''

Kevin Thompson, finance director, notes: ''To recognize our shareholder purpose, we align our staff with the shareholder through remuneration and targeting. We place our employees in positions where they can be successful and have the freedom to take actions and be entrepreneurial. We have forty individual companies and each has a high-quality board of directors. The individuals in charge of those companies are responsible for their success – no excuses. At the head office, we provide the resources. They make the decisions on how their company is run and then they are judged on the outcomes. We align objectives and provide resources so they can make the decisions at their level where there is the most information to make those decisions."

O'Shea expands the philosophy: "Our focus is on results. Our employees find this refreshing. It doesn't matter who you lunched with – it is results that count. This focus has provided powerful benefits in allowing us to retain good people. They like the results orientation because high-quality people do high-quality things. We create alignment of interest. For this reason, we can recruit great people who become very committed to the organization. They feel huge ownership in their operating part. The results orientation is deeply embedded in the culture. It impacts the way people relate to each other. People feel and are genuinely empowered."

"For example," adds Thompson, "managers are judged on their own performance. At times, there may be tensions between companies. We may have a UK manufacturer and a US selling company. Each is trying to get the best performance it can. If there is a quality problem, they don't assume it is someone else's problem – they jump up and down – they see it as their own problem. With the pay focused as it is, this is enforced on every occasion."

"At the head office," O'Shea explains, "we make the choice of markets and businesses. Our business model is focused in safety areas where performance is more important than price. These are long-term growth areas that give our company managers a chance of success. We give them a good basis because of our markets. We are number one in many of our chosen markets because of our long-term relationships that have helped create the industry. Safety markets are long-term growth markets where it is necessary to innovate continually and refresh intellectual capabilities. The common feature of our businesses is their significance to the customer. Often the products are not price-sensitive. They are areas in which it is important to develop intellectual capital. For example, one of our products is a gas monitor for enclosed spaces, which impacts a wide range of industries and where the purchasers' or their colleagues' lives may depend on the product. This product is not cyclical. This is a product where customers care about functionality. We can afford to do R&D. We are rewarded for it. Our customers want us to – and we want to – to be the best supplier in the world."

"And how do we pay people?" asks Thompson. "For our managers, we pay a modest base salary and then an additional reward can be earned if the return in excess of capital is the best that has ever been achieved. We use a value metric that our employees can understand and will create the behaviors we are seeking. That provides a real improvement focus in value terms."

Halma is truly an organization where value leadership is pervasive and integrative. It is part of everything the company does – and all constituents benefit by their commitment to being value-led.

HALMA – KEY INSIGHTS

- » provider of safety products;
- » value-led from the top down;
- » metrics and economic value;
- » strategy;
- » compensation and alignment of interest;
- » providing social and environmental benefits through its products;
- » product excellence;
- » maximizing the value of intellectual capital;
- » running a global organization successfully;
- » using technology to benefit the shareholder;
- » being customers' supplier of choice;
- » garnering market share;
- » R&D investment;
- » results orientation;
- » communications, both internally and externally;
- » shareholder value;
- » a pervasive and integrative way.

Key Concepts and Thinkers

Value-led pioneers and organizations have developed a language which defines value concepts. Get to grips with this lexicon through the *ExpressExec* glossary in this chapter, which also covers:

» key concepts;
» key thinkers.

Activity-based costing – A costing methodology that breaks the costs of an organization down by the activities it performs.

Adding value – See Value creation.

Alignment – Most often refers to the alignment of motivations between capital providers and managers.

Amran, Martha – Co-author of *Real Options: Managing Strategic Investment in an Uncertain World.*

Application service providers – Providers of software online.

Arrogance – According to the *Oxford English Dictionary* " undue assumption of dignity, authority, or knowledge, aggressive conceit ... haughtiness... " Non value-led; indicates either a lack of a firm grasp on reality or too small a vision.

ASP – See Application Service Providers.

Asset pricing – Valuation (pricing) of an asset.

Balanced scorecard – A way of organizing value drivers into groups that make sense to the organization and that attempt to cover the range of possibilities of sources of value.

Beta – A measure of the systematic riskiness of a company's stock. Also called market or non-diversifiable risk since it pertains to the risk associated with the markets in general and not with any particular company's performance.

Bloxham, Eleanor – Author of this text and other works on the topic.

Brealey, Richard – Co-author of *Principles of Corporate Finance.*

Business line reporting – Financial reporting by business area or unit; can be a step that organizations take as they become value-led.

Cannibalism – In Chapter 4, this refers to the extent to which the Internet channel replaces other distribution channels.

Capital – The investment made by others in the business can come in the form of loans (debt) or in the form of a share of the business (equity).

Capital charge – A calculated charge for the use of employed capital. Calculated as the capital multiplied by the cost of capital.

Capital asset pricing model (CAPM) – A financial model that may be used to determine the cost of capital.

Clark, Peter – Co-author of *The Value Mandate: Maximizing Shareholder Value Across the Corporation.*

Cohen, Jerome – Co-author of *Investment Analysis and Portfolio Management.*

Collins, James – Co-author of *Built to Last: Successful Habits of Visionary Companies.*

Commitment – What value-led organizations express in their intentions, thoughts and actions toward value.

Communications – An important part of being value-based with investors and with those inside an organization, in fact, to all constituents.

Conflict – Inevitable in any organization: value-led organizations deal with it openly and honestly.

Continuing value – The value of the firm beyond the time for which it was explicitly forecast or planned.

Continuous improvement – Ongoing improvement in any aspect of an organization; value-led organizations are committed to it.

Cookies – Information sent to a user's personal computer by a website for use by the site during subsequent logins.

Copeland, Tom – Co-author of *Valuation: Measuring and Managing the Value of Companies.*

Corporate governance – The controlling, directing, and regulating of an organization. For corporations, commonly the responsibility of the shareholders, board of directors, and chief executive officer.

Cost of capital – The real (even if not recorded on financial statements) cost of using the capital supplied to the organization by its capital providers. May refer to WACC or cost of either debt or equity capital depending on context; see Cost of debt, or Cost of equity, or WACC.

Cost of debt – Interest cost of debt; may be expressed before or after tax; see also WACC.

Cost of equity – Equity holders' expected return on the capital they have contributed; see also WACC.

CRM – Customer relationship management.

Culture – The way members of the organization interact and/or their expectations about how interactions will operate.

Disclosure – Information provided by an organization. Generally in reference to investors.

Discount rate – The rate at which future cash flows are discounted in order to determine their present value.

Drucker, Peter - Author of numerous important management books including, most recently, *The Essential Drucker: In One Volume The Best of Sixty Years of Peter Drucker's Essential Writings on Management* and *Management Challenges for the 21st Century*.

Eccles, Robert - Co-author of *The Value Reporting Revolution: Moving Beyond the Earnings Game*.

Economic profit or economic value - Measure of the economic return of a firm after including charges for all forms of capital.

Ehrbar, Al - Author of *EVA: The Real Key to Creating Wealth*.

Equity (market) value - The current value of the firm as estimated by the market. Calculated as number of shares outstanding multiplied by share price.

FAS/FASB - Financial Accounting Standards, promulgated by the Financial Accounting Standards Board (FASB), a US non-profit organization, which is the designated organization in the private sector for establishing standards for financial accounting and reporting.

Fiduciary - A person who holds something in trust.

Fiduciary duty - The duty of a fiduciary is to care for and make wise use of the resources held in trust. In this case, the corporate directors have a fiduciary duty to care for the capital invested by shareholders, bondholders, etc.

Financial Accounting Standards Board - See FAS/FASB.

Financial derivatives - A financial instrument "derived" from another financial instrument. For example, a stock option is a derivative of the underlying stock. Derivatives are usually highly leveraged, intangible and risky.

Financial drivers - Those areas of focus in an organization that drive its financial performance.

Goizueta, Robert - Former CEO of Coca-Cola.

Governance - See Corporate Governance.

Government Performance and Results Act - A 1993 action by the US Congress to provide for the establishment of strategic planning and performance measurement in the Federal Government.

Helfert, Erich - Author of *Techniques of Financial Analysis*.

Holistic management - Management of the organization as a whole and not only for financial statement results.

Human capital – Human resources of the firm.

Ideal culture – Culture the organization would like to have.

Information distribution – Use of the Internet to distribute information.

Information gathering – Use of the Internet to gather information.

Innovation – Improvement; new way of thinking about or doing something or the capability of doing something that was not a possibility before.

Internal rate of return – The rate of return attributed to an investment based on future incoming cash flows.

International Corporate Governance Network – An international organization dedicated to promoting good corporate governance.

IRR – See Internal rate of return.

Jarrell, Sherry – Co-author of *Driving Shareholder Value: Value-Building Techniques for Creating Wealth*.

Johnson, Roy – Management consultant and author in the area of value management with a focus on strategy.

Keegan, Mary – Co-author of *The Value Reporting Revolution: Moving Beyond the Earnings Game*.

Knight, James – Author of *Value Based Management: Developing a Systematic Approach to Creating Shareholder Value*.

Koller, Tim – Co-author of *Valuation: Measuring and Managing the Value of Companies*.

Kontes, Peter – Co-author of *The Value Imperative: Managing for Superior Shareholder Returns*.

Koestenbaum, Peter – Author of *Leadership: The Inner Side of Greatness: A Philosophy for Leaders*.

Kulatilaka, Nalin – Co-author of *Real Options: Managing Strategic Investment in an Uncertain World*.

Leadership mind – A term coined by Peter Koestenbaum; includes effectively using vision, reality, ethics and courage.

Leadership will – The combination of ethics, which is the knowledge and desire to take the right actions, and the courage to do so.

Luehrman, Timothy – A visiting associate professor at MIT's Sloan school of management and author on the topic of adjusted present value.

Madden, Bartley – Author of *CFROI Valuation: A Total System Approach to Valuing the Firm*.

Mahoney, William – Executive editor of *Shareholder Value Magazine* and author of *The Active Shareholder: Exercising Your Rights, Increasing Your Profits, and Minimizing Your Risks* and *Investor Relations: The Professional's Guide to Financial Marketing and Communications*.

Mankins, Michael – Co-author of *The Value Imperative: Managing for Superior Shareholder Returns*.

Market risk premium – The rate of return of the overall market over and above the risk-free rate.

Market segmentation – In Chapter 4 this refers to understanding which customers might use which channels.

Market value – The total market value of a company, calculated as the value of debt and equity; see equity value.

Market value added – Calculated as market value less capital.

Martin, John – Co-author of *Value Based Management: The Corporate Response to the Shareholder Revolution*.

McTaggart, James – Co-author of *The Value Imperative: Managing for Superior Shareholder Returns*.

Measurement – A quantification or representation in numerical terms.

Merrin, Roger – Co-author of *Driving Shareholder Value: Value-Building Techniques for Creating Wealth*.

Metric – A particular kind of measurement; see Measurement.

Millstein, Ira – A corporate governance expert.

Minow, Nell – Co-author of *Power and Accountability*, *Corporate Governance*, and *Watching the Watchers: Corporate Governance for the 21st Century*.

Monks, Robert – Author of *The Emperor's Nightingale: Restoring the Integrity of the Corporation in the Age of Shareholder Activism*; co-author of *Power and Accountability*, *Corporate Governance*, and *Watching the Watchers: Corporate Governance for the 21st Century*.

Motivation – The desire to accomplish.

Murrin, Jack – Co-author of *Valuation: Measuring and Managing the Value of Companies*.

Myers Briggs – Widely used personality assessment tool designed by Isabel Briggs Myers and Katharine C. Briggs and based on Carl Jung's explanation of human personality.

Myers, Stewart – Co-author of *Principles of Corporate Finance*.

National Association of Corporate Directors (NACD) – A US organization committed to helping boards improve corporate governance through training and other resources.

National Association of Securities Dealers (NASD) – A US organization committed to providing quality markets and securities regulation. The Nasdaq market is a subsidiary of NASD.

Nell, Stephen – Co-author of *The Value Mandate: Maximizing Shareholder Value Across the Corporation*.

Net present value – The current value of a stream of future cash flows after considering the cost of investments (see also Present value).

O'Byrne, Stephen – Co-author of *EVA and Value Based Management: A Practical Guide to Implementation*.

Open-book management – Coined in the early 1990s, the term refers to the sharing of financial information and providing financial education to employees.

Operating profit – Profits related to the operations of the business, often used to refer to that amount which, less the charge for capital costs, equals economic value.

Options theory – The theory of the relationship between an option and its underlying security. Usually in the context of pricing of the option.

Payback – A simplistic and outdated method of determining an investment's worth by calculating the length of time until the investment has earned back its original value.

Peters, Tom – Author of numerous books, best known as co-author of *In Search of Excellence*.

Petty, J. William – Co-author of *Value Based Management: The Corporate Response to the Shareholder Revolution*.

Phillips, David – Co-author of *The Value Reporting Revolution: Moving Beyond the Earnings Game*.

Porras, Jerry – Co-author of *Built to Last: Successful Habits of Visionary Companies*.

Present value – The current value of a stream of future cash flows (see also Net present value).

Privacy notices – Notices to customers and others informing them of how the organization may use the information which is supplied; a greater issue with the advent of the Internet.

Process improvement – Improvement in an organization's processes.

Raber, Roger – President of NACD (see NACD).

Rappaport, Alfred – Author of *Creating Shareholder Value*.

Regulation FD – Fair Disclosure regulations promulgated by the SEC (see SEC) in 2000; in essence requiring disclosures to all investors at the same time; the purpose is to avoid favored status for certain investors.

Results Act – See Government Performance and Results Act.

Return on assets – Generally calculated as net income divided by total assets.

Return on equity – Generally calculated as net income divided by total equity.

Return on investment – The rate of return on investments or projects.

Revenue attribution – The determination and assignment of revenue to units of the organization, for example divisions.

Rewards and recognition – The entire spectrum of compensation provided to employees including base pay, variable pay, benefits, awards, etc.

Right action – Taking the right action at the right time.

Right intention – The intention to do the right thing. One of the ten elements of a value-led organization.

Right thought – Thoughts in alignment with what is right. One of the ten elements of a value-led organization.

Risk-free rate – Rate of return expected on a riskless asset, generally a US Treasury instrument such as T-bill or T-bond. The definition of *riskless* can be dependent on the time horizon. The yield on a 15 or 30 year Treasury bond is commonly used.

ROA – See Return on assets.

ROE – See Return on equity.

SEC – US Securities and Exchange Commission.

Sharpe ratio – Calculation of the return of a portfolio over the risk-free rate divided by the risk or standard deviation of the portfolio.

Sharpe, William – Author of *Investments* and numerous articles in the area of corporate finance.

Shiely, John – President of Briggs and Stratton and co-author of *The EVA Challenge*.

Sortino ratio – Similar to the Sharpe ratio but measures the excess return over the downside deviation only.

Stakeholder – Any one who has something to gain or lose by the performance or activities of the organization.

Stakeholder activism – Activities of stakeholders with the intent of influencing the organization to act in a way that benefits the stakeholder.

Stated culture – The culture that an organization says it has.

Stern, Joel – Author of *The EVA Challenge*.

Stewardship – The responsible use of an organization's resources by its management. Value-led organizations are good stewards of the resources provided by its constituents.

Stewart, Bennett – Author of *The Quest for Value*.

Strategy value – The value of a strategy.

Stratton, Fred – CEO of Briggs and Stratton and member of the board of directors of Bank One.

Subculture – A sub-unit of a larger culture.

Systematic risk – Market, non-diversifiable risk.

Transaction consummation – In Chapter 4, this refers to the actual completion of transactions on-line.

Transparency – The ability to obtain information about the company so as to see better and to understand what is going on within the firm.

Ublehart, Mark – Consultant and author in the area of value management.

Valuation – Assigning a value to a business.

Value creation – A measure of value created or the act of creating value; creating benefit.

Value destruction – A measure of value destroyed or the act of destroying value; causing harm.

Value leadership – To direct and focus organizational attention on good stewardship and the creation of value.

Value management – The process of managing for value.

Volatility – The amount of variability or risk inherent in an asset or investment.

WACC or Weighted average cost of capital – Weighted after-tax cost of debt and equity capital.

What-if analysis – A form of analysis that seeks to determine the outcomes of several possible scenarios.

Young, David – Co-author of *EVA and Value Based Management: A Practical Guide to Implementation.*

Zeikel, Arthur – Co-author of *Investment Analysis and Portfolio Management.*

Zinbarg, Edward – Co-author of *Investment Analysis and Portfolio Management.*

Resources for Value-led Organizations

There are many excellent reference works which describe value-based philosophies, processes and techniques. This chapter identifies the best resources in books, articles, magazines, and websites on value concepts and on value-led organizations.

This chapter will discuss works important in pursuing the topic of value-led organizations further. Because this topic is multidimensional, the works referred to cover a wide spectrum of views on the topic. For other resources, refer to Chapter 8, which contains a list of key concepts and thinkers.

TEXTBOOKS

Three textbooks are especially useful to students of these topics:

» Brealey, R.A. and Myers, S.C. (1988) *Principles of Corporate Finance*, Third Edition. McGraw-Hill, New York

If one book must be selected, the recommendation would be *Principles of Corporate Finance*. It is a gem and provides an excellent background into the theory of corporate finance as well as discussion areas for further academic research. Comprehensive and easy to read with practical examples, the book begins with value and covers risk, capital budgeting, financing, market efficiency, dividend policy, capital structure, options, debt financing, financial planning, cash management, mergers, international finance, pensions, and the limits of current corporate finance thinking. It is easy to locate topics in this well laid-out text.

» Sharpe, W.F. (1985) *Investments*, Third Edition. Prentice-Hall, Englewood Cliffs, NJ

Investments provides the reader with excellent background on many topics including investment theory, markets, valuation, options, performance measurement and attribution, taxes, leverage, and cost of capital. William Sharpe was one of the people primarily responsible for the theory behind the cost of capital calculation. It includes major concepts with which any value leader should be familiar.

» Cohen, J.B., Zinbarg, E.D. and Zeikel, A. (1987) *Investment Analysis and Portfolio Management*, Fifth Edition. Richard D. Irwin, Inc., Homewood, IL

This book takes the perspectives of analysts and portfolio managers. It discusses key issues of risk and return, how markets work, investment analysis and portfolio management. It also includes in-depth discussions on common stock valuation, industry and company analysis, and valuation of debt instruments and derivatives.

Business and leadership books

» Stewart III, G.B. (1991) *The Quest for Value*. HarperCollins, New York

Nearly 800 pages long, this book provides an excellent framework for understanding value concepts. The book discusses Bennett Stewart's views of how the market works and how it evaluates a firm's results. This discussion provides an underpinning for understanding the nature of capital flows, and that certain firms attract capital and why. It includes a discussion of what investors evaluate. In the chapter on market myths, Stewart discusses some common views of the market and contrasts them with his own.

The book covers the calculations of value in some depth. The examples in the text provide a good understanding of the calculations, why they are made and how to make them. There are several sections that discuss cost of capital, including the relationships between the cost of debt and equity capital. These are worthy of review by anyone wishing to understand these relationships.

In addition, Stewart also discusses early thoughts on compensation. (Although these are early thoughts, they remain important in articulating that compensation can be tied to economic value rather than market value and explaining some of the basic principles that are still used today.)

» Young, S.D. and O'Byrne, S.F. (2001) *EVA® and Value-Based Management: A Practical Guide to Implementation*. McGraw-Hill, New York

This more recent book discusses with great insight and depth the calculations of value from a number of perspectives. In addition, alternative approaches to the calculations are offered and discussed in detail. A useful discussion of the cost of capital provides the reader with some of the practical issues faced in its calculations.

Newer insights on management compensation are also provided. These insights focus on the shortcomings of stock approaches and the beneficial use of value creation methods. There is also a practical discussion of pitfalls in implementations to date, many of which are related to lack of commitment and understanding.

» Madden, B.J. (1999) *CFROI Valuation: A Total System Approach to Valuing the Firm*. Butterworth-Heinemann, Oxford

In *CFROI Valuation*, Bartley Madden discusses cash flow return on investment and the construction of that metric. The book discusses each aspect of the calculation and describes the reasons for its construction in the manner proposed. In general, the focus is on CFROI (cash flow return on investment) as a valuation measurement tool. Like some of the other works, the book considers alternative calculation approaches. The book also demonstrates the benefits of pictorial representations in understanding the numbers.

» Amram, M. and Kulatilaka, N. (1999) *Real Options: Managing Strategic Investment in an Uncertain World*. Harvard Business School Press, Boston

This book provides practical and useful ways to consider and value real business options. In addition to providing ways to address this complex topic, the authors discuss specific examples, including valuing or investing in start-ups, exploring for oil, developing drugs, investing in the firm's infrastructure, and investing to pre-empt competitors. This text takes the information in *Principles of Corporate Finance* and provides many examples and practical applications.

» Copeland, T., Koller, T. and Murrin, J. (1995) *Valuation: Measuring and Managing the Value of Companies*. John Wiley & Sons, Inc., New York

The authors provide in-depth information on how to value a firm and discuss examples of common pitfalls in valuation. This book discusses company value and the manager's mission as well as cash flow valuation.

» Martin, J.D. and Petty, J.W. (2000) *Value Based Management: The Corporate Response to the Shareholder Revolution*. Harvard Business School Press, Boston

This book provides the perspectives of two academicians who survey the landscape of value-based metrics, incentive compensation and management practices. An excellent resource guide to many of the current topics, the book provides information on lessons learned and discusses value-based management and "the imperative for change." The authors also discuss value-based tools for measuring and rewarding corporate performance, and provide their own views on what has and has not worked.

» Stern, J.M and Shiely, J.S., with Ross, I. (2001) *The EVA Challenge: Implementing Value Added Change in an Organization.* John Wiley & Sons Inc., New York

Stern and Shiely discuss the use of value management techniques in areas such as strategy, acquisition analysis and incentives. John Shiely is president of Briggs and Stratton, so the book contains particularly good first-hand descriptions from an executive's perspective.

» Ehrbar, A. (1998) *EVA: The Real Key to Creating Wealth.* John Wiley & Sons Inc., New York

This book looks at value management at a variety of companies, in particular, at Briggs and Stratton, Armstrong World Industries, Boise Cascade and SPX, among others.

» McTaggart, J., Kontes, P. and Mankins, M (1994) *The Value Imperative: Managing for Superior Shareholder Returns.* The Free Press, New York

The Value Imperative discusses value with a strategic perspective. Using strategic principles, the authors discuss the processes that drive value within an organization and what an organization must do to sustain value creation, improve competitive position, and increase market value. This strategic perspective is useful to readers of value-based topics. The book concludes with a noteworthy section on making value creation a core competency.

» Knight, J. (1997) *Value Based Management: Developing a Systematic Approach to Creating Shareholder Value.* McGraw-Hill, New York

James Knight discusses value management and provides useful examples and case histories. The book, written by a compensation strategy consultant, discusses the reasons why managing for value makes a difference and includes discussions on measures, strategy, implementation and pitfalls.

» Rappaport, A. (1998) *Creating Shareholder Value: A Guide for Managers and Investors.* The Free Press, New York

Al Rappaport provides an update to his ground breaking 1986 work. In addition to his insights on business planning, performance evaluation, executive compensation, mergers and acquisition, interpreting stock market signals, and organizational implementation, Rappaport also discusses the relationship between shareholder value and corporate purpose, and discusses the shortcomings of accounting numbers. The book also includes a section on the "The Shareholder Scoreboard" that Rappaport helped to create.

» Monks, R.A.G. (1998) *The Emperor's Nightingale: Restoring the Integrity of the Corporation in the Age of Shareholder Activism.* Addison-Wesley, Reading MA

In *The Emperor's Nightingale* Robert Monks discusses what corporations are and what they can be. He also considers the importance of values in the running of organizations and the important role of accountability to shareholders.

» Monks, R.A.G. and Minow, N. (1992) *Power and Accountability.* HarperCollins, New York

Here, Robert Monks and Nell Minow discuss power and accountability in the modern corporation and how they can be balanced.

» Monks, R.A.G. and Minow, N (1995) *Corporate Governance.* Blackwell, Oxford

Monks and Minow discuss corporate governance, explaining what has gone wrong and the important role institutional investors can play.

» Monks, R.A.G. and Minow, N (1996) *Watching the Watchers: Corporate Governance for the 21st Century.* Blackwell, Oxford

In *Watching the Watchers*, Monks and Minow follow on from *Corporate Governance* and discuss the role of institutional investors further.

» Peters, T. (1988) *In Search of Excellence: Lessons from America's Best Run Companies.* Warner Books, New York

Tom Peters has many important titles. *In Search of Excellence* profiles organizations and cites eight basic principles of management that any organization can use to create value.

» Peters, T. (1989) *A Passion for Excellence: The Leadership Difference.* Warner Books, New York

Here, Peters provides case studies of the passion for integrity, innovation, meeting customer needs, and encouraging employee contributions that are the hallmarks of leadership in value-led organizations.

» Koestenbaum, P. (1991) *Leadership: The Inner Side of Greatness: A Philosophy For Leaders.* Jossey-Bass, San Francisco

Peter Koestenbaum discusses what makes leaders great. As he explains, great leaders have vision, understand reality, and encourage organizational ethics and courage. Koestenbaum discusses the need for greatness in business; the "leadership diamond" of vision, reality, ethics and courage and its application in a variety of spheres. The book provides a wonderful place for value leaders to enhance their own reflective processes.

» Collins, J.C. and Porras, J.I. (1997) *Built to Last: Successful Habits of Visionary Companies*. HarperCollins, New York

In *Built to Last*, James Collins and Jerry Porras discuss visionary companies and what makes them different. Early in the book, they discuss 12 myths and then the key aspects they see in visionary firms. These, they say, include "being a clock builder – an architect, embracing the 'Genius of the And', preserving the core/stimulating progress, and seeking consistent alignment."

Last and certainly not least in terms of books of importance (and there are certainly more that could be discussed but for lack of space), Peter Drucker is well known to everyone in management circles and has many important titles to his credit. Two are worthy of particular mention:

» Drucker, P.F. (2001) *The Essential Drucker: In One Volume The Best of Sixty Years of Peter Drucker's Essential Writings on Management*. HarperBusiness, New York

The Essential Drucker is a compilation by Drucker himself of his most important principles of management, beginning with those found in his 1954 *Management by Objectives and Self Control* all the way through to his latest works. While many of his works are worthy of mention, *Management Challenges for the 21st Century* (HarperBusiness, New York, 2001) is of particular note. It discusses how the paradigms of management have changed and what is now required to be value-led.

MAGAZINE ARTICLES

There are many articles worth reviewing. Listed here are some recent articles of note.

» Luehrman, T. (May–June 1997) "What's it worth?: A general manager's guide to valuation," *Harvard Business Review*

This is one of a series of articles in the *Harvard Business Review* in which Timothy Luehrman discusses the important concept of adjusted present value (APV). This series on corporate finance discusses a topic also covered by Brealey and Myers. What Luehrman does in the articles, however, is to point out practical issues and clearly bring home the advantages of APV in valuation analyses.

» Johnson, R.E. (March–April 2001) "Getting it right: A template for creating real value," *Shareholder Value Magazine*

In this article, Roy Johnson discusses ways to break down value metrics and understand what is driving value.

» Helfert, E.A. (March–April 2001) "Wrong number," *Shareholder Value Magazine*

In this and subsequent articles in *Shareholder Value Magazine*, Erich Helfert discusses the nature of value and the metrics that best support it.

» Mahoney, W. (October–November 2000) "Appraising value beyond the numbers," *Shareholder Value Magazine*

In every issue of *Shareholder Value Magazine*, Bill Mahoney and his staff highlight the most important topics for value-led organizations. In this article, Mahoney discusses the important non-financial variables that drive a firm's value and the importance of organization's "owning" the communication to investors of this key information. In "Measuring the immeasurable" (May–June 2001), Mark Ubelhart discusses the use of value management and provides new insights into the important area of human capital measurement.

» Collins, J. (January 2001) "Level 5 leadership: The triumph of humility and fierce resolve," *Harvard Business Review*

This article, based on a five-year research project, discusses the key attributes of good and great leaders and why they are important in the transformation of an organization.

» Rappaport, A. (March–April 1999) "New thinking on how to link executive pay with performance," *Harvard Business Review*

In this article, Al Rappaport discusses the use of index options.

» Wagner, R.H. (Spring 2001) "Overcoming Stock-Option Addiction," *Executive Talent*

Richard Wagner discusses issues in compensation and the use of options in particular.

The author of this book is also well published in this area. Examples of some of her articles include:

» Bloxham, E. (October 1998) "Why value management," *Journal of Strategic Performance Measurement*
   Discusses what it means to be value-led and the benefits firms can gain by doing so.
» Bloxham, E. (October 1999) "Performance measurement through US binoculars," *Journal of Strategic Performance Measurement*
   Describes cultural issues that impact on an organization's ability to be value-led.
» Bloxham,E. (November 2000) "Intangibles, human capital and options value management," *Journal of Cost Management*
   Discusses important areas of value measurement and focus for value-led organizations.
» Bloxham, E. (Summer 2001) "Rewarding executives who know the score," *Executive Talent*
   Discusses new ways to think about the structure of compensation to maximize value.

MAGAZINES

» *Shareholder Value Magazine* is a great resource publication. It includes examples and issues for value-led organizations.
» *Harvard Business Review*, with its focus on strategy and value, continually offers insights to leaders of value-led organizations.

Other publications of note can be found in Chapter 8. The general business and economic press offer articles on an ongoing basis spotlighting examples of value-led behaviors.

WEBSITES

In the corporate governance area, www.thecorporatelibrary.com is informative and provides a number of links to other websites of interest. Websites are constantly being updated and information can be found by searching for the particular topic using Internet search engines, a listing of which may be found at http://searchenginewatch.com. Searches on any of the authors and items listed in the glossary in Chapter 8 will yield excellent sources of information.

Online booksellers such as Amazon.com and BarnesandNoble.com can also provide information on the latest works. Entering subject categories such as *value* or *leadership* will yield a host of books related to the desired topic. By clicking on a book's title a listing can be obtained of other related books of interest.

The Steps to Making Value-led Organizations Work

- » Every organization can be value-led.
- » The steps to becoming value-led require ethics and courage, which we call "leadership will."
- » An organization should reinforce its actions with the appropriate measures and rewards.
- » There are ten elements that make value-led organizations work.

While the previous chapters, in particular Chapters 4, 5 and 7, have shown examples of organizations being value-led, this chapter will focus on the steps that organizations must take to be value-led in a comprehensive way, and the ten elements that must be in place to make it work.

THE STEPS

The first step any organization must take is recognition. This is an "aha" process, and a choice concerning stewardship. Koestenbaum, in *Leadership: The Inner Side of Greatness* (described more fully in Chapter 9), describes "the leadership mind" as four points on a diamond. These four points are vision, reality, ethics, and courage. The first step to becoming value-led is ethics. Ethics, in this context, includes recognition of the value principles and a desire to carry them out. The next step is the courage to proceed, even if it means breaking new ground to do so.

Together the ethics, which is the knowledge and desire to take the right actions, and the courage to do so, form what I call "leadership will." This "will" is not found in organizations that are not value-led.

Organizations that are not value-led are focused on two extremes of a continuum:

» a focus on quick earnings and a short-term outlook; or
» an organization without purpose or goals for improvement.

The former is associated with organizations that focus their energies on quarter-to-quarter results and engage in very narrow, short-term thinking. The latter describes organizations that are either arrogant (no improvement needed) or apathetic.

To gain the will to be value-led, by contrast, requires several steps. One is understanding what the right actions are. Another is developing a burning desire to foster those actions and the courage to take the actions necessary.

From a practical point of view, the leadership and the board must go through the stages of recognition and understanding (knowledge), desire (motivation) and courage (action bias) to develop the will to move forward in a sustainable fashion.

A good indication of whether the will exists is when:

» the leadership and board clearly understand what is involved; and
» every individual in the leadership team and on the board makes a personal commitment to an active, specific role in the process.

To create that level of commitment or will requires discussion of the ethics and the development of an understanding that moves from mind to heart. When this happens, the desire can then grow so that the courage will be there to take action, and to move outside the traditions, perhaps, to a new way of operating.

When the will is there, it is then time for the leadership and board to form a clear picture of what being value-led means for them. This relates to "vision" on Koestenbaum's diamond. As a follow-on to the earlier recognitions and education, this may also involve a fairly intense education process, developing a clear understanding of what it means to be value-led. This process is likely to include studying many role models from a variety of industries. In this examination, the organization needs to ask itself several questions; if we wish to conduct ourselves with stewardship on this dimension, what does this mean? What would need to be in place for this to happen? Given our culture (see also Chapter 5 for a discussion of culture-related questions to review), what will we need to address? What obstacles may be particular to our situation or our history? As these issues are explored, it may be wise for the leadership and the board to consider input from outside experts who can help the organization to articulate issues that may be consciously or unconsciously buried. These may include issues which:

» the organization would not recognize on its own due to a lack of distanc; and
» may be important to consider but are not generally discussed in-depth in the literature.

This clear picture of a company's brand of value leadership is critically important. For each organization, it will be different. It is important that each board and leadership member owns that picture in his or her own mind, heart, and will.

Once the vision is in place, the next step is to develop a comprehensive plan to bring reality and vision together. This does not mean that the organization will attempt to implement all aspects at once. In fact, the purpose of the plan is to allow the organization to decide where to begin the process. For some organizations, this may be a combination of areas needing a strong turnaround and those where only incremental improvement is required.

Whatever the initial processes, at this stage the organization needs to assign even more specific roles and responsibilities to all board and leadership members. As the plan is pulled together, no one group or area should have all the responsibility for all the effort or its success. And there should be a stake in supporting the others in their endeavors.

To be most successful, the plan should include timelines as well as roles and responsibilities. In addition, the organization should clearly define what success means in each case.

The plan should also document not only what the organization intends to do, but also establish processes to handle obstacles effectively. Having the courage to handle dilemmas that arise is part of being value-led. Establishing the processes within the plan is a first step towards implementation. To become value-led in a pervasive way means the organization must have mechanisms to handle objections and to solicit the best ideas. The board and leadership must recognize that there will always be those that will argue for delay. (For them, it never is the right time.) This is where "will" comes in. The board and leadership must recognize that change will be difficult to some members of the organization. However, the question is, "If not now, when?" And the answer is, "There will never be a better time."

Another reason a plan is so critical is that for change to happen effectively, it must be a priority. Existing initiatives will need to be re-examined. Wherever possible, efforts that would be counter to being value-led must be shut down. In some cases this may be an effort lasting several years. The plan, however, should outline the steps.

An effective plan will need to address not only obstacles, but also specific plans to make sure employees are on board. To do this effectively, the plan should include updates to the recognition and reward mechanisms. The sooner these are addressed, the sooner everyone will be on board. Here again the nay-sayers will say, "It's too soon." Will and courage will be needed to overcome the objections and answer again, "There will never be a better time."

The plan should also include mileposts for accomplishment, celebration and reports to the board. Again, members of the board and leadership should clearly understand this and devote the required time and energy to their oversight responsibility. In the case of the board, specific responsibility for review and comment should be added to the committee charters.

After a broad plan is designed, a specific plan should be developed for each dimension and each unit that will be affected. The organization may wish to choose dimensions and pilot areas where there will be early successes. For these areas, the required recognition and reward structure changes should be outlined. This should include awards, promotions, benefits, and pay-related issues. These changes, ideally, should not only affect the pilot area but all those who are involved in making the plan successful, including the board and leadership. If individuals are allowed the choice of non-participation or non-accountability, the obstacles the organization will face will be much greater and/or the benefits realized will be less.

Measurement should be viewed as an important overall dimension of the plan. Measurement should begin during the learning phases and run through and after the planning phases as well. After the individual plans are formed with descriptive timelines and definitions of success, the organization must develop measurement processes for reporting to the Board and for understanding its own progress. These measures should be both broad and specific. They should also be comprehensive, because what is not measured and rewarded will not receive attention. Chapter 3 and Chapter 6 discuss some of the metrics that the organization should implement. These measures will help the organization to judge its performance and improve its overall processes. In addition, however, measures should include milepost measures of success at a specific level. Process or value driver measures that will relate at specific levels to the overall objective of the dimensions should also be established.

During the learning and assessment phases, "baseline" measures should be established with as much historical context as possible. This context is important because the organization must recognize that progress may not always be straight-line. An assessment of the historical levels of areas to be improved will provide the organization with information about the items within and outside of its control. It will provide information on the potential impacts and forces it may face. This information will be important in determining where the organization is and where it is headed, as well as the steps required to make the plan successful.

The establishment of the measurement processes should be done with a desire for honest appraisal. This is part of the ethical dimension. Without this honest assessment, and without the courage to face reality, the stewardship will not be possible. Supporting the goals should include the appropriate recognition and rewards. Their design is critical to eliminating gaming, dishonesty, and cheating. Their focus should be on the behaviors and improvement that are the hallmark of stewardship. (The Bank One, Odey Asset Management and Halma examples in Chapter 7 describe case studies in this area.) As noted earlier, rewards and recognitions are important dimensions that support an organization's goal of being value-led. Specific reward and recognition criteria should be established to ensure that the plans the organization has outlined are addressed. The reward focus should emphasize improvement on a value basis.

The next step for the organization, of course, is to begin plan implementation. For larger firms, choosing pilots can make sense and selecting the pilot units carefully can be an important factor in driving early successes. If the pilots are not working out, quick analysis will help to determine if the reason is people, or processes, or a combination of both – and what must be done. If a unit proves to be much more difficult than originally planned, two actions should be taken. One, find another pilot that will provide the early successes, employing lessons learned from the initial efforts. Two, work out a new plan for the original pilot. It can be easy to be dissuaded. As mentioned earlier, however, "There will never be a better time."

To learn and to continue to improve, the organization must assess the outcomes and lessons learned from the initial implementation efforts. What has worked? What has failed? To what extent has the organization been reluctant to pursue a new path? Both cultural and process issues must be addressed. It is also important to communicate lessons learned from the implementations. And for the organization to follow through clearly on the rewards and recognition processes, a results orientation is key.

THE ELEMENTS

To be a value-led organization requires that the board and leadership act like leaders. There must be total commitment to the principles of being value-led, to the thoughts, to the conversations and to the actions. Being value-led must become the filter. And to do this requires strong leadership that is confident but not arrogant. Arrogance comes from failure to assess reality properly or failure to develop a large enough vision. To avoid this, organizations must understand what is possible and where they are *vis-à-vis* being value-led. They must be willing to change their minds about the specifics, to continue to learn, but always to adhere to the principles in the best way possible. (See the Odey Asset Management case study in Chapter 7.)

This requires good leadership. The kind of leadership Nell Minow refers to in talks on corporate governance and the board when she says, "Someone has to be the grown up here." To be pervasive, the organization cannot give mixed signals. The commitment of leadership must shine through in their walk and in their talk. First and foremost it must apply to them in their activities and in their rewards. The leadership and board members must be smarter and study harder. In addition to outsiders, they must themselves provide fresh ideas and challenge existing thought patterns.

Since to be value-led means to exercise stewardship, and since stewardship refers to all areas of the organization's endeavor, it means that everyone in the organization must be involved in the process – taking the care, making it better – conscious of each decision.

To be value-led, an organization must be willing to define and follow its own path: to know its own values, to know its mission and to know it in the context of stewardship of all who will be affected.

To succeed, it must develop its own "character." It must be willing to say that it will not take certain actions just because they are expedient. And it must be willing to innovate and experiment, to go beyond where it was yesterday, to where it wishes to be tomorrow.

In summary, then, here are the ten elements that make value-led organizations work:

» Desire, passion and commitment to be value-led;
» Visualization, a focus on character and ethics and a clear picture of what it means to be value-led;
» Right intention in the direction of stewardship and care for everyone affected;
» Right thought and communication focused on being value-led;
» Right action, including actions in alignment with the vision;
» The courage to handle conflict openly and honestly;
» The courage to use honest measurement;
» Rewards in alignment with value creation;
» Continuous improvement and innovation; and
» Continuous learning and effective communication of what has been learned.

Every organization can make the choice to be value-led. Where is your organization on the continuum? What can you do today to make a difference?

Frequently Asked Questions (FAQs)

Q1: What is a value-led organization?

A: See Chapter 2.

Q2: What hurdles do organizations face in becoming value-led?

A: See Chapters 2, 6, 7, and 10.

Q3: How has globalization affected organizations in being value-led?

A: See Chapter 5.

Q4: What issues does the Internet raise for value-led organizations?

A: See Chapter 4.

Q5: Who has contributed significantly to the thought leadership on value-led organizations?

A: See Chapters 3, 6, 8, and 9.

Q6: In what ways are organizations value-led – what are some examples?

A: See Chapter 7.

Q7: Why is it important to understand what a value-led organization is or is not?

A: See Chapter 1.

Q8: What qualities do value organizations have and how do they become value-led?

A: See Chapters 2 and 10.

Q9: What metrics concepts are value-led organizations using and exploring?

A: See Chapter 3, 4, and 6.

Q10: What are the ten elements for success in becoming a value-led organization?

A: See Chapter 10.

Acknowledgements

In writing this book, I am indebted to many people across the globe.

First and foremost, I am indebted to my husband, Robert Bloxham, who was my chief companion in this enterprise, my typist, and my skilful editor.

I am also grateful to Alexandra LaJoux, coauthor of *The Art of M&A: Financing and Refinancing*, who suggested to Richard Burton of Wiley-Capstone that I write *Value-led Organizations*, and to Richard Burton for pursuing her suggestion. I am very appreciative of the work of the editors of this text, Roger Witts and Tom Fryer.

This work includes specific references to people to whom I am indebted for helping me develop and grow my understanding of these topics. In addition, there have been many colleagues who have been of great encouragement to me. I thank them deeply for their support.

For their assistance, in particular, I would like to thank Hugh Hendry and the late James Higgo of Odey Asset Management Ltd., Stephen O'Shea and Kevin Thompson of Halma PLC, and John McCoy, former CEO of Bank One, and to all others, who were so helpful in providing the insights found in Chapter 7.

I thank my parents, Eleanor and John Earle, and my brothers, John and Robert Earle, for their support and encouragement throughout my life.

Above all, my humble thanks and praise to the Creator.

Eleanor Bloxham, September, 2001
ebloxham@thevaluealliance.com

Index

Printed and bound in the UK by
CPI Antony Rowe, Eastbourne

Printed and bound by CPI Group (UK) Ltd, Croydon, CR0 4YY

13/04/2025

14656462-0003